The Limerick Bible

Peter Wallis

The Limerick Bible

Copyright ©Peter Wallis 2005

First published for Peter Wallis in 2004 under the title "There once was a word from the Lord" by Verité CM Ltd. 2nd edition published in 2005 by Verité CM Ltd, 124 Sea Place Worthing, West Sussex BN12 4BG. Tel: 01903 241975. www.veritecm.com

A catalogue of this book is available from the British Library

ISBN 1-904726-43-7

Typesetting and design by Verité CM

Printed in the United Kingdom

ABOUT THE AUTHOR

Peter Wallis was born in a quiet suburb of South East London during World War II in a bedroom above his father's dental surgery. Soon after that there was an air raid, but there is no published evidence that any of those three facts were in anyway inter-related… or is this little book, which has appeared 60 years after those events, the key to another of God's chuckles?

Most of Peter's schooling was at Monkton Combe, near Bath. He graduated in Medicine at King's College, University of London, and King's College Hospital Medical School. He eventually entered General Practice – at first in South London (without air raids) and then for 25 years in West Sussex. Having been a Reader in the Anglican Diocese of Chichester, to his surprise he found himself called to ordained ministry. He trained at S.T.E.T.S. at Sarum College in Salisbury, delved deep into a filing cabinet containing his A.K.C. certificate from his days at King's College, London, and was ordained at Chichester Cathedral at St Petertide 2001.

Having retired from General Practice he now serves as N.S.M. priest in the villages of Yapton, Ford and Clymping.

Peter is married to Davina, they have two grown up children and four grandchildren.

PREFACE

'The Limerick Bible'

How did this little book come to be written? The honest answer is that it was an accumulation of indignation, inspiration, and challenge.

Indignation that a colleague had been dismissive of "Limericks" in general, and of their appropriateness to the proclamation of the gospel of Jesus Christ in particular.

Inspiration from various sources that gave impetus to the view that the thoughts came originally from the Holy Spirit, even if they got a bit murky on the way.

Challenge that the only way to see if it could be done was to attempt it, and then subject it to crushing criticism – which may be one of the good reasons for reading it anyway!

It was never my intention to make a "translation" of the Biblical text into "Limerick form", but rather that I should retell some of the Bible stories and sayings to facilitate enjoyment of the Bible, to encourage the reader to go back to the script, and to find out for themselves what God has said.

I believe that all poetry (that is pure, primitive or profound) is a gift to us so that we may receive enjoyment, encouragement, and a deeper experience of God. I do hope that this approach to the Holy Scriptures will give many readers a taste of the sweetness of the simplicity of God's word, and thereby be tempted to discover the excitement and hilarity which are ours for the asking. (1 Corinthians 1: 18-25)

Felpham, W. Sussex, The Feast of All Saints, November 2003

From the Bishop of Horsham

Oh the best book to read is the Bible!
The best book to read is the Bible!
If you read it every day,
It will help you on your way,
Oh the best book to read is the Bible!

Some people will go to extreme lengths to encourage others to 'read, mark, learn and inwardly digest' the Scriptures. Peter Wallis is one such. It's because he believes the Bible is God's Word, standing over and above any of the countless other words spoken, written, listened to or read in human history, that he has taken a risk by daring to 'limerick' the sacred text.

This delightful book is a taster, a lovely and accessible introduction to some of the stories and personalities that leap from every page of the Bible. It will make you wonder. If it is the 'best' book to 'help you on your way', as the limerick I sang as a child suggests, the Bible is not an easy read. Words 'crack and slip and slide' as they speak of truths too deep for words.

Peter's delightful doggerel honours the Word, not least Peter himself honours it. He is a man of God. That's my experience of him over many years, though I might say that when I ordained him a priest, I knew not of this particular talent for rhyme.

I read the whole lot in one sitting! And my favourite five lines?

There once was a sheep that got lost,
But his shepherd, discounting the cost
Searched the land till he'd found him,
Put a safe fence around him,
And with all of his friends, he rejoiced.

This says it all...

Lindsay Urwin OGS

 *The Limerick Bible*

ACKNOWLEDGEMENTS

I am very grateful to my wife, Davina, for her thorough reading of the text, and for her editorial advice, particularly when the sublime exceeded the ridiculous.

Thanks to Mrs Young of Accurate Secretarial who typed (and retyped) the script.

I would like to record my gratitude to Verité CM Ltd for their encouragement and advice.

And finally, my thanks to my good friend David Houghton for picking up the omissions and errors that no one else spotted.

P.W.

DEDICATION

For my grandchildren Ben and Samantha,
Charlie and Lucy

And for their parents, Debs and Paul,
David and Sally

There once was a word from the Lord
That in 'limerick' format was stored
Whilst it made easy reading
The profound deeper meaning
Was by God himself whispered and roared.

So read on, and see if you find
God's great secret is merely confined
To concise little stories
Or perhaps rather more is
Just one tale that makes you opine

Genesis - Beginnings

There once was a person called "God",
Who considered it really quite odd
That some folk adored Him,
Whilst others ignored Him
And called Him a silly old bod.

So God said, "Some stories I'll tell
So that people might know me quite well"
And some tales were hairy,
Some charming, some scary;
There were also some strange ones as well.

The Creation Story

It's in Genesis where it all starts:
God created it all in six parts.
It was good, so He blessed it,
On day seven He rested
And for ever His love He imparts.

At the start, not a semblance of form:
Utter chaos was seen as the norm
And the face of the deep
Lay in turbulent sleep:
A new era was soon to be born.

Old Testament

Then a nuclear seismic eruption
That was global, intense and caused ruction
Turned dead mass to matter
Making bright lights and clatter
To all this the Lord gave His unction.

The sky, and the seas, and dry land
Was the next group of things that He'd planned;
"Now for plants we shall need
Either rhizone or seed"
Said the Lord, "It's so good and so grand!"

Next came fish in the rivers and seas
And the birds that could fly with great ease
And reptiles, and mammals
(Some were quaint like humped camels)
And God looked on it all, and was pleased.

The climax of God's whole creation
Was called 'human' and lived as one nation.
For Adam and Eve,
(We are lead to believe),
Completed God's perfect equation.

The Garden of Eden

God had planted a garden in Eden
Which was gorgeous, and needed no weeding.
And the man and his wife
Had the time of their lives
And met up with the Lord every evening.

"There is only one rule you need know"
Said the Lord, their creator "Don't go
Near the fruit of that tree
It's exclusive for me
If you eat it, you'll die (Eve said Oh!)"

The Garden of Eden was bliss,
It was here where Eve had her first kiss.
She made Adam a coat
From a pre-deceased goat
Adam stared at it, asking "What's this?"

The terrible truth then sunk in:
Eve had picked a banned fruit, and the skin
As it peeled off, sprayed juice
(that was their sad excuse)
Turning all of their innocence to sin.

That which God had denied them, they had,
But instead of new rapture, just sad
Loveless boring existence
That put a vast distance
Both between each other and God.

For now that they knew they were naked
(Which they said was caused by what the snake did)
God quickly made clothes
That would cover their toes
And make them more cautious, less raked.

From Eden at once they were banished
The garden just totally vanished
And all Adam's descendants
Showed interdependence
That was loveless and badly mismanaged.

Eve and Adam were blessed in due season
The birth of two sons was the reason
The great interaction
Of sexual attraction
Meant conception's best chance they should seize on.

Their sons they called Abel and Cain,
The lads argued and fought all in vain
Now whilst Cain dug the soil
He failed to find oil
But Abel kept sheep on the plane.

But alas! little filial love
Was extended by Cain to his bruv',
For the elder bro' Cain
Who was jealous and vain
Got his own way by push and by shove.

Each brother decided to bring
To the Lord God a thank offering
"To God – it's from Abel"
For thus read the label
Cain's comment: "I'm not bothering."

Cain's complacency angered the Lord
How dare he assume God had poured
His blessing paternal
On that which was vernal
Thus Cain's off'ring God tot'lly ignored.

Then Cain murdered his brother, and lied,
His punishment shattered his pride
He was sent off to Nod –
Without morals or God –
And he stayed there until he died.

A conscience God gave Adam and Eve
And a means by which they could believe
In a Great God of love
Who they could not quite prove
But who promised them He'd never leave.

In due course, all types of behaviour
Broke the ways of the Lord, thus a saviour
Was the perfect solution
And only conclusion
For this reason the Covenant God gave you.

Adam's manly third son was called Seth
He lived a long time till his death.
On Cain fell God's vengeance
(which rarely got mentions)
Except in disdain by his wife.

It was then, that the scriptures imply
That men called on the Lord to ask "Why?"
Life seemed void of all meaning
Many hours were spent dreaming
About pie in the sky when you die.

The Story of Noah and The Ark

Things continued to go hopelessly wrong
For away from the Lord folk had gone,
So God whispered to Noah,
"I'll send down a shower
That'll last about forty days long."

Then God said to Noah, "Be shrewd!
Build an ark, even if folk are rude
Take two of each creature -
I'll make sure they won't eat you
And I'll make you a really cool dude."

Of Noah, it was said, he was righteous
Whilst building the ark he p'raps might just
Have queried the need
For the size and the speed
Of construction techniques that were choicest.

Noah filled up the ark to the brink,
Which created a terrible stink!
Noah's wife disliked reptiles,
And banned pterodactyls;
And that's why they're all now extinct.

Many weeks the ark sailed on the flood
Before running aground with a thud.
Noah then sent out a raven
To find a good haven
That wasn't all covered in mud.

Noah also sent out a white dove
(This bird's now a symbol of love)
Each day the dove searched
For a place it could perch
Then returned with a twig from an olive.

When the earth once again was quite dry
God said, "Never again will I try
To destroy my creation
And to show my intention
A rainbow I'll place in the sky."

And these were the very good reasons
Why the Lord God created the seasons
"Tell each creature – 'Go Forth'
– East and west, south and north,
Multiply and restock the depletions.

The family of Noah increased quickly
Genesis ten lists well over fifty
There was Nimrod the hunter
And Canaan the grunter
Their combined skills had made them quite nifty.

In those days they all lived long lives
And Enoch, we note, never dies
The oldest, Methuselah
(Not to confuse you, though)
Topped nine-sixty-nine- Quelle Surprise!

A descendant of Noah was called Cush
Who always went round in a rush
His son was called Nimrod
And he was no dim bod
Like a hunter who leaps bush to bush.

When Chedor-Laomer was king
His pugnacity helped him to win
He slaughtered in Sodom
Grabbed Lot by his bottom
But his army got coated with bitumen.

The Story of The Tower of Babel

The story of Babel is how a
Group decided to build a huge tower:
To reach heav'n by themselves
And find just where God dwells
Would give them, they thought, all His power.

The tower was a work of precision
That failed due to human derision
Of God's perfect planning
That didn't leave man in
Ultimate charge of decisions.

When the Lord saw just what, and how much
They'd achieved without training as such
He said "Their one language
Would cause them great anguish
If they all start to speak Double Dutch."

The Appearance of Abram
(whose name was later changed to Abraham)

Now creation was still in a mess
So Abram God chose to bless.
God's promise propitious
Was in no way capricious,
But surprised Abraham none-the-less.

The first time that God spoke to Abram
He revealed to him what was his plan:
That Abram was blessed
Both in goods and with zest
His descendants would round the world span.

Sarai, who was Abram's first wife
Was a beautiful woman – so nice
The fellows admired her
The Pharaoh desired her
Which caused some embarrassing strife.

The Lord came again to see Abram
And confirmed all the details were plain
God said, "I've changed your names
For real – it's no game
From now on it's Sarah and Abraham.

King Melchizedek, priest-king of Salem
Made a banquet especially for Abram;
Then Melchizedek blessed
All that Abram possessed:
The covenant now would not fail them.

What is "The Covenant?"

The OT spends time in explaining
That it's simply agreement pertaining
To the special relationship
Like a containership
Binds in as one those remaining.

The Covenant itself was tripartite
The name change affirmed they'd departed
For whilst "Abram" deferred
To his origins in Ur
"Abraham" meant a new age had started.

Abraham's faith is commended by Paul -
Romans 4:13 on says it all;
Then the ratification
Of the Lord's one oblation
Is the means by which "might" becomes "shall".

Sarah likewise, by Paul was commended
For her faith, once dishevelled, now mended:
She provides an example
Of faith rendered ample
And real – that which once was pretended.

King Abimelech

King Abimelech made a mistake
When he made up his mind that he'd make
Sarah into his wife:
But the fright of his life
Was when God, in a dream made him quake

"Sarah's Abraham's wife", the Lord warned
"And you'll die if my precepts are scorned.
Yes, she's sort of his sister -
If you really insist a
Close search how the family's formed."

Abimelech asked Abraham why
On earth he could let him e'en try
To court her and marry her
Then be labelled "bad character"
Ostracised until he might die.

Abraham replied "I was so scared
That you'd kill me if it appeared
That we were man and wife
For the rest of our life"
After which King Abim' disappeared.

The Story of Lot

Abram's nephew, a young man called Lot
Was well known for the huge herd he'd got
He recalled that he'd seen a
Large plane that was greener
To move there would be his best shot.

But the people who lived in the land he
Had moved to were raucous and randy;
The morals of Sodom
Were right at rock bottom
And Gomorrah was known as quite dandy.

A volcano blew up at Gomorrah
Leaving Sodom devoid of tomorrow
Lot's wife came to a halt
And at once turned to salt
Which caused all of them fear, shock, and horror.

Thus again Abram came to the rescue
To Lot, he said "I'd like to ask you
Please, as you gain wealth
Make sure it's no stealth
And you'll find people come to respect you.

Now it's Abraham

When Abraham first lived at Mamre
It seemed that it was most unlikely
That Sarah would ever
Conceive a son, "Never
Mind," she said, "I'll do it my way."

A servant of Sarah's called Hagar
Was drawn into a plan that could make her
A surrogate mother
With minimal bother -
It was just up to Abraham to take her.

The plan worked, and Hagar conceived
"Here's your son" Hagar said, "Aren't you
pleased?"
But the plan had backfired
Sarah, angry and tired
Screamed, "Take him and go – you are freed."

Sometime later three angels appeared
"We've good news for Abr'am," they cheered!
"Cos next time he kisses
His lucky ole' missus
She'll get whassnamed – don't never you fear."

Sarah laughed at this angel's bad joke
How unkind to speak thus to her bloke!
Though she eavesdropped the tent
She was sure what was meant -
She'd heard clearly each word that he spoke.

Sarah laughed – she was post-menopausal
But the Angel of God said, "Of course he'll
Restore her fertility
And her ability
To God that is just a mere morsel.

Sure enough, just about a year later
Little Isaac appeared, and his Pater
Showed him off to his friends
Saying, God always sends
His solutions, but very much later.

Then with Abraham, God made a deal
And to demonstrate that it was real
God said, "If circumcision
You perform with precision
Then you'll find it's no trouble to heal.

Now Ishmael was also a son
Of great Abraham. "What have I done
Wept his desolate mother
For I did nothing other
Than what I was told should be fun".

For many long years, though the first born
Young Ishmael was subject to much scorn
His name means "God hears"
There was anger and tears
With his kinsmen he always was war-torn.

The Twins

Isaac's birth brought much pain and much
laughter
But in childhood there came near disaster;
A vast sacrifice
Was to be the huge price
And Isaac was marked to be martyr.

Isaac became father of twins,
And would jest that the first born would win
All his wealth, and his flocks,
(Of which there were lots)
Number two was then left not a thing!

But the second son's skills were in dealing,
And for breeding the herd, he had feeling,
This slippery young lad
(Nick-named 'Jacob the bad')
To his mother was much more appealing.

Jacob's mother helped Jacob to swindle
His brother's eventual windfall
Jacob ran off to hide
With his uncle's huge tribe
And a friendship with Rachel was kindled

Leah and Rachel, the daughters of Laban,
Were keen to inherit, but knew no man
Whose precise antecedents
Had just the ingredients -
Until Jacob arrived – they said, "Stay, man!"

Israel the Man... Israel the Nation

It was Jacob who founded genetics
Though his style was devoid of all ethics
His family extended,
His future depended
On cunning and nomadic methods

He had many sons, and some daughters;
"The Children of Israel, they call us"
Explained one of the tribes
Who was quite used to the jibes
At the size of the land "that God bought us"

For through Jacob began an expansion
Of a tribe far too big for one mansion;
A nomadic people
Who managed to keep all
The best for the Israelite nation.

Many decades had passed before Esau
And Jacob were reconciled. Each saw
The mutual benefit
In times where any fit
Young King tribesman might go off to war

Whilst at Bethel (known also as Luz)
Jacob had a quick nap, (as one does)
As he peacefully slept
In his dreaming he met
Angels climbing up stairs – like a bus

When he'd reached the top of this ladder
He realised then how God had had a
Desire to affirm him
Which thrilled and perturbed him
On reflection, it made his heart gladder

The name 'Jacob' meant 'I'm a deceiver',
But the neighbouring tribes all said 'He's a
Shrewd and astute man
Just like Father Abraham,
In whose God he's the greatest believer.

On the night before Jacob met Esau
He was startled by what he thought he saw
A man just appeared
(And this was quite weird)
He grabbed his leg making his knee sore.

The two of them wrestled all night
By dawn they were still in the fight
The man touched his hip
But still kept his lips
Shut – so Jacob yelled "This isn't right."

"Who are you, and what do you want?"
The man replied, "I have been sent
To rename you Israel
And call this place Peniel
For that was the Lord God's intent.

Joseph the Dreamer

Now whilst Jacob was shrewd and a schemer
The twelfth of his sons was a dreamer
Who embarrassed his family
And made his bro's angry
And said a lot more than he need do.

To enhance this precocious lad's ego
His Dad made him a coat that was yellow
And red, blue, and green -
The most garish robe seen
It reminded one more of a rainbow.

To cut a long story quite short
This lad Joseph made his brothers fraught
Then, by cunning and knavery
He was sold into slavery
And about him his family forgot.

Joseph found himself stuck in a slave-market
It was quite the most dreadful thing he'd known
yet
He was sold to Lord Potiphar
Whose wife said "Now what if your
Duties we worked out in bed?"

When he heard his wife's felonious tale
Lord Potiphar threw him in jail
Joseph realised the verdict
Was flawed – every word it
Contained made the youngster go pale..

For allegedly lecherous behaviour
The sentence in jail did not waiver
The young Jo had to go
In to prison, and so
He had no hope of seeking a favour.

Sometime later, the butler and baker
Of the Pharoah were jailed by mistake – er -
They both had strange dreams
Which to Joseph, it seems
Would turn baker to own undertaker?

Soon the butler was back in his pantry
The baker was hung in the gantry
But young Joseph excelled
In the post he now held
And mixed well with the top 'gyptian gentry.

Years later a famine caused Israel
To find somewhere else for their cereal
They migrated south
Till they reached the Nile's mouth
Where th' Egyptian power reigned quite imperial.

By this time, young Jo was P.M.
There was no-one more powerful than him,
Except for the Pharoah,
But he'd left affairs to
That very same Joseph – yes, him!

With delight Joseph met with his brothers
His father, and several stepmothers
He booked them all in
At the Pharaoh's best inn
And said, "Now you'll be free of all troubles."

The Exodus:
The story of Moses and the Children of Israel

Israel's family then moved to the Nile
Stayed on holiday there for a while;
After four hundred years
All their fun turned to tears
For they no longer lived there in style.

The Children of Israel lost status
Whereas once they were guests, now were waiters
The Egyptian high flyers
Called them social pariahs
And bragged they were firm Hebrew haters.

Very soon they had no social standing
The Pharaoh was shrewd in his handling
Of this turbulent tribe
Whom he thought he could bribe
By his shouting, and raving and ranting.

Then he swore that he'd make their tasks harder
"Make the bricks without straw" – a disaster
The time then was ripe
To save Israel, – God might
Use some foul plagues to get them out faster.

Now young Moses was Hebrew by birth
But of Coptic young males there was a dearth
Moses clever shrewd Mum
Found a way that her son
Got the best education on earth.

The Pharaoh of Egypt was evil
And demanded the Hebrews must leave all
The male babies born
To a fate so forlorn
That you'd never, not ever believed it all.

Pharaoh's daughter it was who had found him
In a basket with pitch all around him
Moses very own Mum
Was persuaded to come
To the palace as nurse – how astounding!

Moses also was thought to be violent:
He'd once killed an Egyptian assailant
Of a helpless young Hebrew
That he thought no-one knew
But word still got round: he stayed silent.

It was thought best if Moses just went
Before Pharaoh's police got the scent
So he first stayed with Jethro
(Which saved him from "Death Row")
And learned about livestock instead.

Jethro's daughter took a fancy to Moses
It was not long before he proposes
But details of their wedding
Are locked up in heaven
Which stopped journalistic imposers.

Now the Exodus tells about Moses,
Who was warming his cold little toeses
By a bush that was burning,
Which gave him a yearning
To think about questions God poses.

God said, "Moses, I want you to lead -
Go to Pharaoh for Israel to plead"
Moses said, "I've a stutter..."
God said, "That doesn't matter,
What I want is that Israel is freed."

Moses asked of the Lord "Who's the boss?
I've no name I can call you, because
You said you could only
Be seen by the holy
But what that means, I'm at a loss."

Then God said "I AM WHO I AM
There is no other name that you can
Tell my people to call me
And to bow down before me
For JEHOVAH or YAHWEH I AM."

The plan to free Israel from Egypt
Was to start with a closely kept secret;
But a plague or two later
That Egyptian Dictator
Was only too pleased to agree it.

A list of the plagues sounds like fiction
One long horror film full of affliction
What with rivers of blood
And giant frogs in the mud
And locust and flies – all Egyptian.

The ultimate plague would be death
Of each firstborn male that was left.
The next morning all Egypt
Groaned when they perceived it
Had left them completely bereft.

That the "Angel of death" had passed over
The Hebrew homes was the disclosure
That the Passover meal
Was symbolic and real
And was eaten with solemn composure.

The ingredients were: bread with no yeast,
(As a symbol of how this strange feast
Was consumed in a hurry)
Cooked with tart herbs -no curry
And roast lamb, a male firstborn at least.

Free of blemish or any deformity
The one-year-old firstborn lamb had to be;
Then vicariously slain
So that it bore all the pain
Of the people whom God now would set free.

The blood of the sacrificed lamb
Was smeared on the door and the jamb.
The angels of hell
Were unable to tell
Any other suggestion or plan.

The significance of this strange party
Devoid of enjoyment and laughter
Would not be apparent
Till a deeper inherent
Explanation followed long after.

Without compass or map or instructions
The Israelites seemed bent on destruction
On this cumbersome trek
Many Hebrews said, "Heck
How on earth shall we guess which direction?"

So the Lord set a pillar of cloud
In the sky which for certain allowed
Every person to see it
Then they all could agree it
And progress on their way very proud.

A pillar of fire by night
Made their campsite secure, safe, and bright.
The horsemen of Egypt
Gave chase till the Red Sea bit
Where they drowned, and all vanished from sight.

The Israelites crossed the Red Sea
And thereafter continued to be
Disgruntled complainers,
Despite daily manna
And quails in abundance for tea.

As they wandered through Sinai's waste
Moses realised they needed to taste
The goodness of God
Which they found rather hard
As they moved on from place on to place.

The idea of a moveable temple
Seemed an ideal solution, quite simple;
So Aaron's team looked
Through the tentmaker's book -
Who was skilled with resources quite ample?

There once were two skilful designers
Who used to make seats and recliners
Oholiab and Bezalel
Were always pleased to tell
"There's no-one makes these any finer".

With Ithamar, they had overall charge
Of constructing a Tabernacle, large
Enough for the altar -
A design without falter
Which looked like a marquee-cum-cage.

When the vestments and ark were completed
Yet again the Israelites cheated;
They complained that their government
Endangered their covenant
And their food was bad – they couldn't eat it.

The Lord God was angry with Israel
He asked Moses "Why are they so miserable?
As for that rabble
They're nothing but trouble
But if they repent, I'll forgive them all".

The people continued to moan,
So round Sinai they had to roam
For years – about forty
Had made them less haughty;
The Promised Land then they were shown.

Ten commandments God gave them to follow
That would outlast their every tomorrow
Moses wrote them all down
On large tablets of stone,
Which they all said were too hard to swallow.

But while Moses was up on the mountain
The Children of Israel were counting
How much gold they had got
To throw in the pot
And then turn out a calf to bow down to.

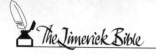

Moses came down the mount with "The Law"
He was angry and sad when he saw
What his brother had done
In pursuit of good fun –
What would happen now, he wasn't sure.

There once was a man, name of Korah
Who stirred people up, saying "You're a
Great bunch of God's people
So why should you not keep all
The worship in your style and manner".

"By what right does this Moses and Aaron
Insist that the priests keep their hair long
And other such trivia
That bodes ill for living here
Vote them out – we'll take care when they've all gone."

So they met at the Tent of the Meeting
Moses stood there whilst Korah was speaking
Korah's tribe and supporters
Their sons and their daughters
All fell silent – perturbed by loud creaking.

The earth around Korah gaped wide
The rebels all started to slide
Down a vast deep ravine
(Now they'll never be seen)
That was the price for their pride.

The Book of the Law - Leviticus

Now Leviticus sets out the Law;
The rules number six hundred or more;
But they're there for a reason,
To ignore them is treason,
But to read them straight through is a bore.

The priests all came from the same tribe
Which caused an occasional jibe
The Levite integrity
Was their priority
Not ever did they accept bribes.

Leviticus speaks of atonement
As something that is of great moment:
The role of the priests
Was to keep all the feasts
That honour the Lord God's enthronement.

The Book of Numbers

In Numbers it tells of a donkey
Who behaved like an ill-mannered monkey;
For this sage of an ass
Made a very rude pass,
And told Balaam, "You're prophecy's wonky!"

The Book of Deuteronomy

In the book that is called Deuteronomy
God said, "Moses, tell Israel I'm gonna be
Very angry and sore
If they don't keep my law
And continually love me and honour me".

The Exodus started with Moses;
Deuteronomy tells as it closes
That Moses had died
But no search far or wide
Would reveal where his body reposes.

The Book of Joshua:
The Promised Land

On the East bank of Jordan they stood
And wondered how ever they would
Cross that murky old river;
But God was the giver
Of the where-with-all by which they could.

Reports by the spies were quite glowing:
"It's a land that is rich, and is flowing
With milk and with honey,"
Said the son of Jephunneh
Replied Joshua, "Right, lets get going".

There once was a hooker in Jericho
Known to her neighbours as Rahab-the-pro,
Because she told lies
And protected the spies
She was saved when the walls fell-in-one-go.

So the Israelites took over the land
They fought Jericho with a brass band
At Ai, defeated
By treasure secreted,
The rest of the conquest – as planned.

Joshua summoned the Israelite nation
And spoke out for the next generations
As his life's end drew near
Many leaders shed tears
And confirmed that from God came salvation.

At the end of his days, the old general
Insisted that he spoke to them all
He said "Each one must choose
Who to stand by or lose,
As for his house, they'd all serve the Lord".

General Joshua died of old age;
To the Israelites, he'd been a sage
He was followed by judges
Who listened to grudges -
Some quite good ones appeared at this stage.

The Book of the Tales of the Judges

At the start of the book of the Judges
It is clear that there were many grudges
Between differing clans
With no definite plans
Though God frequently sent hints and nudges.

King Jabed of Canaan caused pain
His cruelty had earned him a name
For twenty long years
He'd brought Israel to tears
And it looked like he'd done it again.

His army was championed by Sisera
Who enquired of the people "Now is there a
Lady who might
Bring me special delight?"
Answered Jael "Come with me – you'll not miss her".

So into her tent Jael enticed
The general – he went out like a light
Then Jael took a hammer
Through his skull she then rammed a
Large tent-peg. He died. Well he might.

Then Barak joined Deborah in song
(There were thirty-three verses – quite long)
But despite the swashbuckling
Component, the chuckling
Confirmed that God's victory was won.

It seems strange, in the twenty-first century,
To read of the crude deeds all meant to be
In honour of God,
From those who through blood
Seek out violence before claiming victory.

Now Jephthah from Gilead was stronger
And braver than any war-monger
Who might try to insult him
Or otherwise fault him,
And age-wise looked younger and younger.

On the way back from victory he vowed
In a voice that was raucous and loud
That he'd kill the first person
He saw – which was worse than
He thought – T'was his daughter – he howled.

She smiled sweetly, and led the parade
Unaware of just what she defrayed
For her life was the price
Of the mad sacrifice
For which Jephthah received accolade.

Deborah

A beautiful prophet called Deborah
(Which means "honey-bee" not a zebra)
Was persuaded to sing
To the Lord God, her King,
A song of rejoicing for ever.

The Story of Gideon

A timorous fellow called Gideon
Was God's choice in the downfall of Midian
Using smashed jars and cheers,
Grasping torches, not spears
Gideon's Israelite army got rid of them.

The Story of Samson

There once was a strong man called Samson
Who was rugged and hairy, and handsome
His strength, it appeared
Was concealed in his beard,
Which, if shaved, risked his being held ransom.

The story of Samson's great weakness
Might be titled "The Strength and the
Sweetness"
For the lifestyle he donned
Quite resembled James Bond
Surrounded by girls for completeness.

Now Samson was known as a poser
To the ladies he liked to get closer
As they fondled his hair,
They would ask of him "Where
Does your strength arise – tell me, O please, Sir."

Then he met up with Delilah
Her beauty was such, he desired her
She asked for some locks
Of his hair – the old fox
Samson guessed the request was contrived, though.

But when Samson, obsessed with Delilah
Lay down in her bedroom beside her
He found his prowess
Landed him in a mess
For the source of his strength, he'd supplied her.

The Philistines had a surprise
For poor Samson – they gouged out his eyes
Then in Dagon's huge temple
They said, "It's quite simple -
We'll torture him now till he dies!"

But the Lord heard this libertine's prayer
And his strength was restored then and there
He smashed the whole building,
Which killed them – and killed him,
And thus he died bravely – with flair.

Judges Chapter 19

Now in Judges, in chapter nineteen
Comes the weirdest of tales that has been
Recorded in Scripture,
For this one is richer,
And stranger, and, frankly, obscene.

The Story of Ruth

But the story of Ruth's a romance
That will send you right off in a trance
It caused young girls to swoon
Long before "Mills and Boon",
Reading how Ruth caught Boaz's glance.

Hannah - Mother of Samuel

There was a devout lady called Hannah
Who each year, with her husband Elkanah
Attended the temple
For prayer, pure and simple
And then she'd return home to Ramah.

Her problem was one of fertility
The priest asked her "What can the matter be?"
She explained her predicament
And told the priest her intent
"In a year" he said "OK that'll be."

Within the one year she gave birth
To a son, who grew up to be worth
His God-given calling
To challenge the appalling
National spiritual dearth.

Samuel, Kings and Chronicles

Then in Chronicles, Samuel, and Kings
Are recorded a number of things
About good kings and bad 'uns,
And how God's heart gladdens
When in worship, his praises folk sing.

The Story of David and Goliath

The acromegalic Goliath
Caused Israel a great deal of strife
Cried this giant of a champ
From the Philistine camp,
"Now who'll come and fight for their life?"

The Israelite army of Saul
Had no suitable champion at all;
But the young son of Jesse
Told everyone, "Yes he
Would deal with the giant once for all".

He declined King Saul's offer of armour,
Saying "No-one could possibly harm a
Young chap with a sling
That he'd happened to bring"
Which made everyone feel a lot calmer.

The lad picked five stones from a brook;
With precision and skill David took
Careful aim at the giant
Who remained quite defiant,
And with cynical laughter he shook.

Seconds later, Goliath was dead
The Philistines all shook with dread
Though the pebble was little,
The giant's skull was brittle,
And the stone swiftly pierced through his head.

David then on was hailed as a star,
His fame spread from near and from far
But the mighty King Saul
Didn't like it at all
Saying, "What a young upstart you are!"

David and Jonathan

A deep friendship grew up between
King Saul's son, and the lad who'd been
Crowned in Saul's place
After Saul had disgraced
The priestly authority supreme.

The truth that lies 'neath the sad tale
Is that good in the end must prevail
And that friendship and love
Can surpass flesh and blood
And make strong that which might else be frail.

The Downfall of King Saul

Saul forfeited his title of "King"
By doing a terrible thing
When Samuel the Priest
Was late for the feast
Saul sacrificed the burnt-offering.

David is Crowned King in his place

To Bethlehem Samuel then fled;
Searched out Jesse, just like God had said;
Told him, "Bring me your boys,
For the one of God's choice
Is going to be crowned King, instead".

So Samuel anointed young David;
From then on the young lad was favoured
With skill as a soldier,
Thus, as he grew older
Attempts on his life were evaded.

The Tale of Nabal

There once was a fellow called Nabal
Who thought he was skilful and able
And handsome and cool.
He was really a fool,
And appeared in an old book of fable.

He decided to give a wild party
But got drunk and became far too hearty
He fell into a coma,
His face looked like a stoma
He died without dignity – nasty.

Nabal's wife was a lass known as Abigail
Who's sweetness and charm never seemed to fail
Of the swift death of Nabal
She was really unable
To grieve, or show sorrow, or weep and wail.

King David then comforted she
Who's dear husband was Nabal, you see,
Her affections soon rallied,
And quickly she married
King David, as wife number three.

The Tale of Bathsheba

A dreadful adulterous deed
Was the sin of King David, when he'd
Seduced young Bathsheba,
And then planned to keep her -
Uriah, he had killed out of greed.

But a prophet called Nathan exposed
The King's hypocritical pose
King David repented
For seven days lamented
The lesson? 'You reaps what you sows'.

Samuel

Now Samuel was the last of the Judges
Of whom some had been good, despite smudges
Or flaws that portrayed their
Extraordinary behaviour
And dubious motives and urges.

But Samuel was clearly God's prophet
Any scheme he thought wrong "Hey come off it"
He would say
In a most awesome way
That ensured the proponent would drop it.

He had crowned as their king mighty Saul
And been with him until his great fall
With the ascent of King David
His importance then faded
When he died, he was mourned by all Israel.

Mephibosheth

Sometime later King David enquired
Was there anyone not yet expired
Of the family of Saul
On whom we could call
To ensure that Saul's lineage survived.

A grandson of Saul called Mephibosheth
Had in childhood experienced "near death"
It could have been worse
He was saved by his nurse
But alas she fell crushing him none-the-less.

The injuries that he sustained
Made it seem like he always felt pain
Just the thought of a Zimmer
Would make him look thinner
But his gait would remain much the same.

So up to the "Table Royale"
Summoned personally, ventured the loyal
Son of Jonathon, who
Really had little clue
Why it was he was not made to toil.

When Samuel died, the entire nation
Were in mourning without hesitation
But Saul found a medium
(He'd been told he'd no need of them)
The message was "Extermination".

The first book of Samuel's about Saul
Of his height and good looks: most of all
That God's Spirit forsook him -
He'd no time to look in
To how he marked this as his fall.

Samuel two tells the story of David
From the time of Saul's death, he behaved as if
The whole land was his own:
And when not on his throne
He never forgot that God gave it.

The Death of King David

King David was really quite old
When despite all precautions, a cold
Turned to double pneumonia
From there it was only a
Question of time: his eyes closed.

When he died, he had reigned forty years
Eventful at times full of tears
And sometimes some sorrows,
But all his tomorrows
Brought back victory rather than fears.

Just prior to the death of King David
Each of his sons said "I'm the favourite
Therefore, I should be King
In succession to him"
Their anger and scheming got rabid.

So King David determined to place
The son of his choice in that space
"It shall be King Solomon"
(He'd said that's so, all along)
The other sons left in disgrace.

At Jerusalem, greatest of cities
King David wrote most of his ditties
He called them "The Psalms"
For they deal with life's qualms
And the way that God loves, cares, and pities.

PSALMS AND WISDOM

The Songs of Zion

The Psalms are a mixture of songs:
Some are short, others really quite long
But whilst lots sing God's praises,
Some ask, "Why the blazes
Does God, with replies, take so long?"

The Psalm that is shortest of all
Is a psalm that, despite being small
Says "Extol Him, you people !
With loud voice that's not feeble
And for certain He'll hear when you call."

The longest psalm (that's one-one-nine)
In each stanza, provides for a line
That tells of the light
To guide and delight
Those who follow close by all the time

The twenty-third Psalm was a favourite
The tune "Crimond", they said, was just made for it
But the Vicar of Dibly
(whose own tune was not giggly)
Asked how much it had cost and who'd played for it.

King Solomon

King Solomon built a huge temple:
In size and décor – monumental,
His neighbour, King Hiram
Asked "What had inspired him?"
It was awesome, and made people tremble.

He had also created a palace
A magnificent building that was
A great Courtroom of Justice
Where wisdom and trust is
Dispensed without bias or malice.

The great Queen of Sheba herself
Decided to see if his wealth
And his wisdom so famous
Was merely cutaneous
Or deep and profound, free from stealth.

Her visit went down in history
As one political mystery
King and Queen were attracted:
But no treaties extracted:
Whatever's to be, is to be.

Famed for his wisdom was Solomon
His love-life inspired him to write a song:
For the names of his wives
And his harems besides
Makes the longest such list that you'll come upon.

The Proverbs

The Proverbs are words to the wise
That only a fool would despise,
They include a description
Of what 'er in the kitchen
Can achieve if she works hard, and tries.

Wisdom is played by a lady
Whose social standing p'raps maybe
The best in society
Complete with propriety
She influences ever so ably.

To the lazy she says "Look at the ant
How industrious and loyal – now why can't
You be guided to follow
The Lord's way – don't wallow
In sin, but ask God what he wants."

There's a song that's quite clearly erotic -
Every version of Scripture has got it!
King Solomon wrote it,
(On the ladies he doted!)
And no censor's attempted to cut it.

The great lover was also the preacher -
"Ecclesiastes" he wrote, "So's to teach you
That glamour is fragile,
It soon dies in exile
When 'good things' no longer can reach you".

"Ecclesiasticus" urges that honour
And praises be lavished upon a
Doctor whose healing's
A gift most appealing,
And saves you from being a gonna.

The Houses of Judah and Israel

After Solomon died, his great kingdom
Was divided in two, and a ding-dong
Of fighting and skirmish
Continued in earnest
Between Judah and Israel. Both won.

Many legends surrounded the future
Just a few are included to suit you
Jeroboam for starters
Was in no way as smart as
Rehoboam and his style "Haute couture".

Job: A Study in suffering

Poor old Job had recurrent bad luck;
You'd have thought in the towel he might chuck
His three friends were all pains
Who, again and again
Said, "With you, Job doth stoppeth the buck!"

As Job faced yet another calamity
He might well have questioned his sanity
His patience was ended
He no longer pretended
That what he'd held dear was just vanity.

Even then he believed "His Redeemer"
Would be in the end his "deliverer"
But 'til then his righteousness
Was held through God's good grace:
His sufferings then stayed – but extremer.

Kings and Chronicles again

The prophet Elijah appeared
Without warning, in 1 Kings, and jeered
At that slimy King Ahab,
(For with Jezebel, he had
Said, "No longer need YAHWEH be feared")

Of Elijah, the prophet is told
A story that's really quite bold
In the village of Zarapeth
(Which is quite close to Nazareth)
Lived a widow with son – not that old.

A famine had ruined the land
And the village had never been grand
But Elijah each day
Prayed that there they might stay
Though the reason they'd not understand

Catastrophe struck – the lad died
The widow with grief was beside
Herself. But she trusted
Elijah, who must have
Some clue what to do – like a guide.

The prophet with care took the lad
To an upstairs room – he looked so sad;
But with Cardiac Massage
And Airways – clear passage
The heart was restarted by Gad!

Elijah the Prophet

A parallel tale of Elisha
Makes the reader bemused, and despite a
Convincing conclusion,
There remains some confusion
In the way that both stories surprise you.

Now the prophets of Baal had all been
Constant and loyal to the Queen;
But the cause of the drought
They just could not find out,
Which cost them their treasured esteem.

Elijah suggested a duel:
The winning God from then on would rule
"So come up Mount Carmel
For surely no harm'll
Befall you," he said, "And stay cool".

Baal's Prophets all climbed with Elijah
And killed a large bull right beside of
The altar and pyre
That was untouched by fire:
This was going to be a decider!

All the terrified prophets of Baal
Screamed and shouted, and started to wail
Now whilst Baal remained silent
His prophets got violent,
But Baal looked quite certain to fail.

Then Elijah the prophet took charge
And, calming the frenzied priests' rage,
He said, "I think we ought to
Soak this lot in water -
Twelve jugs full should do, I would gauge?"

Then Elijah said just a short prayer
And before he had finished, the air
With wild flames and bright flashes
Spewed out red hot ashes,
And Baal's prophets all gasped with despair.

That sacrifice burnt to a cinder
Baal's prophets ran trying to find a
Safe place to hide -
But the lot of them died
Outright, or were fatally injured.

About now the thought struck Elisha
"Who would take on the mantle of Elijah?"
Elijah said "If
When I go, you are with
Me, the Lord will then be your provider".

Naboth's Vineyard

In Jezreel the best vineyard of all
Was quite close to King Ahab's grand hall;
It was Naboth who owned it
At no time he loaned it
Round the edge was a splendid brick wall.

Ahab often walked past these fine vines
He already had sampled the wines;
The more Ahab desired it
And tried to acquire it
The more Naboth said, 'No! It is mine.'

Ahab whinged, and Queen Jezebel burst
'You're the king, if you want it you've first
Refusal, you see –
Let two scoundrels agree
That they swore God by Naboth was cursed.

The result was just as the queen planned
Naboth's protests 'Not Guilty' were slammed
The crowds killed him by stoning
Completely disowning
The perversion of justice in hand.

More about Kings

The reigns of the Israelite kings
Were noted for different things:
Whilst the stories of Judah
Make a narrative you'd have
Thought would make warning bells ring.

Like "1066 and all that"
Many tales they kept under their hats
The kings were passed "Good"
Or "Evil": they could
List them under the "Secrecy Act".

There was a young king called Jehoshaphat
Who took care of his feet lest they should go flat
He avoided the sword
And he followed the Lord
As all good kings should do, and so that was that.

King Jehoshaphat went into battle
With King Ahab, who started to rattle
With great apprehension
He quite failed to mention
He'd planned a disguise "Fool them, that'll".

The fighting became very fierce
When an arrow at random clean pierced
King Ahab's aorta
Which leaked blood and water
By the evening, Ahab was deceased.

After Ahab, the Kings were a mixture
Some were good, some were bad, some
perplexed yer
Some reigned on for ages,
And became wise old sages -
A royal and permanent fixture.

When King Jehu took over at last
He drove with great fury, and fast
He only went slowly
When he passed places holy
But he'd never let anyone past.

The Story of Naaman

There once was a General called Naaman,
Who said very clearly he'd pay a man
If he could cure his disease
Put his mind right at ease,
And avoid any needless strict army-men.

His fear was he'd contracted leprosy
Which was swiftly apparent for all to see;
He was sent to the prophet
Whose advice Naaman scoffed at
"Go and wash in the Jordan – d'you see?"

Eventually he did as he was told
Though the Jordan was murky and cold
Seven times he went in
Which cured flesh, nerve and skin
And from which a true faith evolved.

Asa

There once was a good king called Asa
Whose mother did things that disgraced her
Her idols were crude
In fact, downright rude
In the end they just had to replace her.

From the thirty-ninth year of his reign
King Asa began to complain
Of bad pain in his feet
Which caused loud indiscreet
Language to match the bad pain.

But never did he seek out a cure
Nor ask God for something obscure
Nor self-medicate lotion
Nor try any potion
That might make attacks of pain fewer.

When he died he'd one foot in his grave
That had been there a while so's to save
Just some of the suffering
About which he was muttering
The people still thought him so brave.

Jabez

There was a young fellow called Jabez
Who always did that which the Lord says;
He asked God for a lot
And that's what he got
Because he obeyed the Lord always.

Hezekiah

Hezekiah was politically restive
To his courtiers he said "It is best if
We continue in neutral
(I hope that will suit you all)
And avoid being overtly festive.

Hezekiah was a bright engineer
With a great gift of making things clear
The need for fresh water
Was something they ought to
Respect and hold very dear.

He was also a man of great piety
Who ruled in Jerusalem quietly
But Sennacherib, with rage
Locked him up in a cage
With instructions to maintain security.

King Joash

When King Joash discovered "The Law"
He complained he'd not seen it before
Then he led the whole nation
In humble contrition,
And they vowed that the Lord they'd adore.

Then he ordered a Passover feast
Of roast lamb, and of bread without yeast;
The whole celebration
Was quite a sensation –
In charge was Hilkiah, the priest.

There followed a series of kings,
Who got up to all manner of things
Their lifestyles were heinous
And sometimes ingenious
To survive all political swings.

But after a considerable while
They all ended up in exile;
Their defences just cracked;
Jerusalem was sacked,
And the land was a ruinous pile.

Israel's Exile in Babylon

It was Cyrus the King of all Persia,
Before he completed his first year
Of reign, had decided
That God had provided
An ever increasing inertia.

It was God's plan to reverse the exile
Though his people complained, for some while
Their prayers of contrition
Found fulfilment of mission:
The captives returned in grand style.

Ezra

Ezra compiled many lists
To ascertain "who still exists
As a priest (bona fide):
Only those of whom I say
Your genealogy fits".

The foreman of works was Zerubbabel
Whose brief was to rebuild the temple wall
Ezra's task was much broader -
He must watch for marauders
And defend all the workmen as well.

It was Ezra who rebuilt the walls in
Jerusalem, when they had fallen
Into gross disrepair:
Ezra made it his prayer
And his life's work, devotion, and calling.

Nehemiah

There once was a man whose expression
Spoke of worsening, chronic depression
Why his face was so glum
Was a mystery to some,
But the King made a one-off concession.

The King asked this doleful Israeli
For a full explanation why daily
His austere grave apparel
Was as dull as a barrel,
When as cup-bearer, he should have smiled gaily.

Nehemiah replied "I am so blest
That the King hears my plight without jest"
Then he told of the exile,
(his speech took quite some while)
But the King wished to do what was best.

Artaxerxes, great king of all Persia
Was keen there'd be no lost inertia
But the greatest fatigue
Came from political intrigue
When Sanballat contrived more dispersion.

The connivance of Nehemiah's foes
Was powerless to overcome those
Who believed that this vintner
Had been led by God into
A brand new career – there it goes!

The tale is a story of trust,
Of faith to obey – that's a must
For despite opposition
From drab politicians
Nehemiah's brave project won – just!

Esther

There once was a Jewess called Esther
Whose beauty was noted when quests for
The loveliest maidens,
Who were groomed in the harems
Ensuring that none could molest her.

Queen Esther, once, so it is said
Posed seductively, lying in bed
The King was quite taken,
The court was quite shaken
Her beauty had gone to his head.

Quite innocently, Esther discovered
A foul plan, soon to be uncovered
To rob from the Jews
And then to carouse
Taking care that their own nests were feathered.

Mordecai, (Queens uncle), decided
That a wonderful chance God provided
When the Queen heard just what
Was the terrible plot
That to her had by chance been provided.

The chief plotter was none less than Haman
The king's own and trusted right hand man
"Ethnic cleansing of Jews"
Was the theme he would choose
To present to the king a worthwhile plan.

The Queen of King Ahasuerus
Asked, "Would he be pleased to declare as
A festival night
When all wrongs are put right
And his enemies cry will be 'Spare us'".

But through the skill of the queen and her uncle
Careful planning prevented a bungle
Mordecai was spared
And the Emperor declared
"Haman shall hang – the carbuncle!"

The Story of Daniel and his Friends

A devout young Israeli called Daniel
Was ear-marked for tasks that weren't manual
When the king had his dreams
Only Daniel, it seems,
Could explain them, but only post-prandial.

This same Daniel was fed to the lions
His legs had been shackled in irons;
But the lions said they'd spare him -
They'd gone vegetarian
And thought they were all just great try-ons.

The Emperor, Nebuchadnezzar,
Known as king of all kings (so's to impress you)
Had a dream quite prophetic
And vivid, but yet it's
Significance caused deep displeasure.

68

The advisors in things astrological
Failed in every attempt to explain it all
The question that foxed them
(which they complained mocked them)
Was "Did the King dream a strange dream at all?"

The gift of profound understanding
Led to Daniel's fame quickly expanding;
But as makers of history
Unravelling mystery
Daniel and friends were outstanding.

"In the dream," great King "N" was a statue
Made of gold – quite the largest one that you
Will have seen, to this day,
But with feet made of clay
Risked collapse at a single sneeze "Aaatchooo".

King N. made an image of gold
And insisted the nation was told
To bow down to this idol
(Non-compliance-suicidal -
Cremation whilst living – that's bold!).

Abednego, and Mishael and Shadrach
Were found praying to God in a police check;
They were thrown in the fire
But they did not expire
And the plan was dismissed as a reject.

Nebuchadnezzar went on having dreams
That caused his nocturnal bad screams:
He saw a fine tree
That was destined to be
Stripped and hacked using crude and cruel means.

With great terror, the dream was explained
Despite warnings, the King failed to contain
His arrogant pride
Thus he'd now be deprived
Of his empire, and heritable claims.

King N. was deposed from his throne
And was left in a field all alone;
Whilst various physicians
Took up differing positions
Whether 'fitness to rule' could be shown.

King N's illness was labelled 'psychotic'
Though no-one could say how he got it
At one stage, in Syria
It was thought that 'porphyria'
Could have caused it, but so could 'narcotics'.

After Nebuchadnezzar had died
His son king Belshazzar took pride
In debasing behaviour
Which caused a bad flavour
And political unrest, besides.

This truncated youth, King Belshazzar
Threw a banquet, designed to give pleasure;
But a hand that appeared
Wrote in script (that was weird)
On the wall where the king kept his treasures.

Only Daniel, throughout the whole nation
Could provide a quite certain translation
The King's senior doctor
Noted how very shocked were
The guests who'd had hallucinations.

For the king what it said was no thrill;
It reduced the king's kudos to nil
"King B. you fall short of
The standards you ought've
Kept foremost – this night you'll be killed".

The Prophets

Isaiah

When the prophet Isaiah gets a mention
Theologians soon raise the question
"Just how many there were -
Was it one, two, or more?"
But their arguments fail from perdition.

Isaiah's roots were aristocratic
His religious beliefs quite thematic;
But Isaiah chapter six
Finds Isaiah in a fix
When his ideas of God went frenetic.

The year that King Uzziah died
Was the year when to God Isaiah cried
"O Lord, make me holy -
But ever so slowly,
'cos I've got funny feelings inside".

The book of the prophet Isaiah
Foretells of the coming Messiah;
Like a child and a King,
Fresh new hope he would bring
And a living perspective inspire.

Isaiah speaks of God's servant, who brings
A new national outlook on things;
There will come a redeemer
Whose self-sacrifice seems a
Way out for the problem of sin.

Jeremiah

Jeremiah was a talented poet
Though his family and friends didn't know it
He wrote odes about scarecrows,
And blacksmiths and bellows;
People hoped that he would not outgrow it.

Jeremiah went down to the potter's
To see if perhaps he had got a
Nice jug he could take
To the people and break
It, and tell them that they were all rotters.

"Lamentations" by young Jeremiah
Is a poem that's bound to inspire
The reader to think
That he stands on the brink
Of despondency dreadful and dire.

But there's hope by the end of the poem
That can help you to see where you're going
So stay in there in faith,
Or you'll end up a wraith,
And wonder whatever you're doing.

Ezekiel

For his breakfast, Ezekiel had scrolls,
Which made quite a change from bread rolls
These were followed by wheels
Which let off eerie squeals,
And folk wondered, "just what are his goals?"

When Ezekiel was told he must shave
He was cautioned that he must be brave
Then the word from the Lord
Said: "To shave, use a sword,
But take care, or you'll end in a grave!"

The sword caused extensive disaster
Lacerations required sticky plaster
Whilst cuts deep and wide
Needed stitches to hide
The damage – not trivial – much vaster.

That God's love and God's justice are equal
Was a theme of the prophet Ezekiel;
Was Ezekiel psychotic?
Or in fact had he got it?
We shall just have to wait for the sequel.

Meanwhile, back in the vale of dry bones
No movement, no creaking, no groans;
Not a semblance of life
Not the least sign of strife
Ezekiel is puzzled, and moans.

Then into the bones the Lord breathes:
The prophet was brought to his knees
An army appeared -
It was all very weird
And he wondered what God would achieve?

The Twelve Minor Prophets

The Old Testament ends with twelve prophets,
Each one was quite certain just what it
Was that they should preach,
And whom they should reach,
Then make sure that their hearers had got it.

Hosea

The wife of Hosea was a hooker,
  Though it's said she was quite a good looker
But Hosea loved her more
Than just any old whore,
Never once, was it said "He forsook her".

The adulterous life-style of Gomer
Would have made any husband disown her
But Hosea's devotion
Was as wide as the ocean,
And as deep as the whole works of Homer.

Then Hosea told the people, "You're whores!
You've offended Jehovah, because
You condone all that's evil
And refuse to believe all
The word of the Lord and his laws.

Amos

A herdsman who came from Tekoa
  Said "It's just like it was when old Noah
Built an ark – but the nation
Rejected salvation,
And dropped all their morals much lower.

Joel

"The Day of the Lord" is the theme
That this prophet was sent to proclaim
Yet again they rejected
The evidence collected
Which showed just how evil they'd been.

'The Day of the Lord' brought disaster,
It could not, in fact, have been nastier
But remembering His covenant
Despite the corrupt government
Intervention by God came hastier.

Obadiah

Obadiah shook the kingdom of Edom,
And warned that they'd lose all their freedom
Whilst others, like Micah
Told Judah, "God's like a
Great Judge who is eager to pardon".

Jonah

That the Lord had called Jonah to Joppa
Was not true, it was just a big woppa
That caused a great storm
Which made Jonah forlorn,
And dream he'd invented the "Choppa".

The reason that Jonah was smelly
Was because he'd got stuck in the belly
Of a very large fish,
Which had not been his wish
But turned both his legs into jelly.

Jonah preached on "Repentance" at Nineveh,
For the people were all in a hell-of-a
Huge moral mess,
That caused spiritual distress
And some sociological bother.

Micah

Micah pictures the Lord God on trial
Whilst the villains are freed for a while
This quite ludicrous court
Then accedes that it ought
Off its face wipe its complacent smile.

For the prophet speaks up for the Lord
And the truth of his trustworthy word
Restoration is coming
And the people are running
In penitence back to their God.

Nahum

The prophecies spoken by Nahum
Warned strongly that soon there'd be mayhem
Defeat of great Nineveh
Would release untold limit of
Armed forces who'd capture and slay 'em.

Habakkuk

The theme of the prophet Habakkuk
Was depression that caused him to pack up;
But the Lord sternly thundered,
"You need not have wondered -
I'll show you there's no need to crack up".

Zephaniah

A royal prince was the young Zephaniah,
Descended from King Hezekiah,
His prophecies tell us
That our God is jealous,
For his love for his children's like fire.

Haggai

Haggai wrote only one book,
Which, though short, is well worth a good look;
Encouragement is sent
Because he's intent
That the word of the Lord's not forsook!

Zechariah

Zechariah was both prophet and priest,
His eight visions rekindled a quest
For purification
Throughout the whole nation
Which for certain would please the Lord best.

Malachi

With Malachi, prophecy ceased
For a while, though God still spoke through priests
The O.T. was ending:
The Lord God was sending
A kingdom of love, joy, and yeast!

A Pause for Reflection

Thus the path of the covenant stretches
Right from Abraham to exile it vexes
The Lord who is faithful
To see how disgraceful
And sad were his children – such wretches.

Taking a wider view of the Gospels

That the Gospels of Matthew, Mark, Luke
Are quite similar is really no fluke,
For their clever friend, Q
Told them what they must do
To ensure that they each wrote a book.

St. Matthew wrote his for the Jews,
St. Mark wrote that people might choose
To read Mark and learn,
If to God they would turn
He'd accept them, and never refuse.

St. Luke wrote his gospel, and Acts,
Which records with great care all the facts
For his good friend Theophilus
To understand why it was
The gospel stopped folk in their tracks.

The mystical gospel of John
Begins with a beautiful song
Of the Word and the Light
Both given that we might
Walk closer with God, and grow strong.

John's gospel speaks further of light,
And of blindness replaced with full sight
It tells of rebirth
And how Jesus conversed
When he met Nicodemus by night.

New Testament

The story unfolds like a serial -
The details are quite immaterial
Changing water to wine
Was just simply a sign
Of a gospel superbly ethereal.

The Birth of Jesus

St. Luke tells the "Christmas card" story;
About angels, and choirs singing "Glory
To God on the highest"
And "Peace – for the Christ is
The hope of the nations that shall be".

Chapter one of his treatise begins
With two songs that all Christendom sings
Chapter Two has two more
And an angelic choir
Enough to make heaven's bells ring.

The tradition of Christ in the manger
Was a symbol of God as a stranger
With no Bethlehem base
No luggage – no case
It was rumoured he might be in danger.

On the eighth day was Christ's circumcision
The naming? unanimous decision
"He is Jesus", they said
Thinking forwards instead
Of backwards for false inspiration.

They went up to the temple from Bethlehem
Where an old man called Simeon met them
(He'd been told he'd survive there
Till he'd seen the Messiah)
Now he took the babe gently, and blessed them.

The prophetess Anna, rejoicing
Came over to speak aloud, voicing
A word from the Lord
That this child of accord
Would bring in a new Israel – surprising?

When his parents came home from the Temple
They began to perceive what a shamble
They could offer as "Home"
To the Christ of the throne
And yet how he did not dissemble.

The family moved to a "chippy"
(For woodwork, not fried chips and fishes)
Mary's young husband Joe
Taught him "All that he knows" -
J.C.'s going to be skilled and nifty!

Luke and the Music of the Gospels

St. Luke has a passion for music
And obviously chose to include it
Thinking "What if a singer
Was also the bringer
Of the gospel" "Receive don't eschew it".

Thus you'll find in Luke's gospel some songs
Linking covenant and people who long
To broadcast the story
Which tells of God's glory
For Immanuel our saviour has come.

Zechariah sings first "The Benedictus"
To remind us that God is still with us
He's been there from the start
And gives light to the path
Of God's people; hope is what he gives us.

The singing of Mary, Christ's mother
Was so pure and unmatched by another
"My soul will give praise
To the Ancient of Days…"
The Magnificat soars way above her.

The song of the angels sends shivers
Of joy down your spine as it hits us
With amazement, as Simeon
In full voice sings "Now its time"
And that's how we have "Nunc Dimittis".

It's of note that the birth of the Saviour
Traces back the great tales of God's favour;
In the ancestry listed
The author's insisted
On including all sorts of behaviour.

The Arrival of the Wise Men

St. Matthew records how wise men
Set out towards Jerusalem
Though their info was good
They just misunderstood
That they should have been heading for Bethl'hem.

The result? they were some two years late
But their guiding star for them did wait
Such relief when they saw it
They could not ignore it
For it led to the child pure and great.

They brought gifts that were fit for a king
They gave frankincense fresh as a spring
For a child two years old
They brought huge lumps of gold
But the myrrh really wasn't the thing.

Then all of them had a strange dream
"Get to Egypt, and quick, for it seems
King Herod's annoyed
He is quite paranoid
And what he now plans is obscene".

The message from God was quite clear,
The angel had said "Disappear"
So off went the Magi
And so did the family
But in Ramah just screams could you hear.

Sometime later an angel appeared
To Joseph, and said "The coast's cleared"
So they came back to Galilee -
In Nazareth Joe thought he'd be
A self-employed chippie – they cheered.

Jesus is 12
his parents take him to the temple

When Jesus was just twelve years old
They decided that he should be told
The full story of those
That the world calls "The Jews"
A people left out in the cold.

With his parents he went to Jerusalem
The Passover feast was not new to him
But as they returned
They very soon learned
That Jesus was missing – they'd look for him.

It wasn't just teenage behaviour
They had lost God's dear Son, manhood's saviour
But they need not have worried
Nor so anxiously hurried
For with man and with God he'd found favour.

In the temple they found their lost lad
"We've been searching the city, we had
All but despaired
Did you not think we cared?"
Asked his parents, now relieved and so glad.

18 years later...

John the Baptist and the Baptism of Jesus

In the desert lived John the Baptiser
Whose diet was quite a surprise, for
On locusts and honey
He lived (without money)
And people around him got wiser.

On the banks of the old Jordan river
John the Baptist took care to deliver
A call for repentance
Which really was meant as
A call to respond, and not dither.

The baptismal ministry of John
Explained all the mystery song
Of Isaiah chapter forty
It made folk think, "Now ought I
Be baptised, and freed from my wrongs?"

People spoke about John the Baptist
Strong in faith, and in muscle, and wrist
But he said, "Someone greater
Than I am will later
Live among you: for real he exists".

But when Jesus asked John to baptise him
A voice from the sky quite surprised him
"This man is my son
And I'm proud, for he's done
What I asked – so obey, don't despise him."

King Herod viewed John with disparage –
He'd spoken against Herod's marriage
To his brother's ex-wife
Which was sure to cause strife
But did little for Herod's poor courage.

Then in prison without sentence or crime
John the Baptist just whiled away time
He wondered, "How long?"
Like the psalmists sad song
For the prison was far from sublime.

At a sumptuous feast, young Salome
Danced her way round the ball-room alone –
she'd
Intrigued all the guests
Who asked, "What's coming next?"
She said, " 'Tis up to King Herod to show me".

"Anyway," she said, "What does it matter?
King Herod's getting older and fatter,
I might as well get
The most dreadful thing yet
"I want John the B's head on a platter!"

The Temptation of Jesus

Then Jesus was whisked out of sight
To a desolate place, where he might
Be tempted past caring
In agony bearing
The devil's best efforts at spite.

But not once did the Lord Christ succumb
To the hideous schemes that would come
From the devil alone
As he fought for God's throne
But failed through the name of his Son.

The devil then had an idea
Which he said (at a stroke) would both clear
Hunger and all pollution
Such a simple solution –
"Fresh bread for the world, and free beer."

For a split second Jesus stayed silent
Then in clearest of speech, but not violent
Said "Have you not read?
Man shall not live by bread
Alone, but by the word that God sent".

To Jerusalem next they both went
A spectacular jump, the intent
Thought of by the devil:
A divine ropeless abseil
Off the top of the temple, he meant.

He misquoted the psalms when he said
"You'll not injure one hair of your head"
So have faith, Jesus, try it,
You might quite enjoy it"
Jesus said, "Get behind me" – he fled.

"Worship me, worship me, worship me"
Screeched the devil "and there's bound to be
Total world domination
For no other nation
Except yours – try it now, and you'll see".

"God's alone is the only authority
It is there, not by vote nor majority"
Said Jesus "Now go
And this you should know
This is God's world, and for ever shall be".

The devil stomped off in a huff
For a while he'd had quite enough
Jesus went back to Galilee
Found twelve good friends that he
Thought would stay with him though it be rough.

Jesus at the Synagogue

To the synagogue he was invited:
To read from the scriptures delighted;
The Lord could choose what
Part of Isaiah he got:
The people became quite excited.

"The Spirit of God I've received,
He's anointed me, that I believe
To bring to the poor
God's good news – and what's more
The captives, they'll all soon be freed.

The blind will receive back their sight
And no longer will those of great might
Flaunt exclusive behaviour
For the year of God's favour
Will be mighty, and free from all strife."

Jesus rolled up the scroll and looked round;
Were the people expecting profound
And sublime moral teaching?
Or would such stark preaching
Revivalist leanings confound?

The whole town spoke highly of Jesus
Though some remained cautious, "For he's just
The carpenter's lad,
Who works for his Dad -
What he says might not always quite please us."

Changing fishermen to fishers of men

Jesus saw several friends who'd been fishing
"Follow me" he smiled "soon you'll be wishing
That you'd let down your nets,
'Cos who follows me gets
A place on the Kingdom's great mission".

It was Andrew who first saw the light
He thought to himself "Jesus might
Be the one whom we're seeking
Listen now when he's speaking
His ambiance seems about right".

Simon Peter was next one to join
Quickly followed by James and young John
Others said "Count me in"
As did Thomas the twin
But he still wondered "Is it a con?"

The next day, Jesus went up to Galilee
He found Philip and said to him, "Follow me!"
Off went Philip – fetched Nathaniel
Who asked them "How can you all
Be sure he's O.K.?" "Come and see!"

When Matthew signed up to be "Treasurer"
Some cheekily asked him "How much is there
Of cash in the kitty"
His reply (rather witty)
"There's enough for our needs – what a pleasure!"

The number of friends grew and grew
But the Lord knew just what he would do
Instead of an oratory
He gave them authority
To preach and to heal and renew.

The miracles of Jesus from the start of his ministry

The first miracle was Jesus' own birth
And the way that he entered this earth:
For His one incarnation
Sufficed for each nation -
And heaven rejoiced with great mirth.

After being baptised in the Jordan,
Jesus' ministry started – according
To Isaiah the prophet
Who Mark says has got it
Correct and concise in his wording.

Jesus changed water into wine

The wedding in Cana of Galilee

A village called Cana-in-Galilee
Was a proud and respected community
When a wedding was announced
All the caterers pounced
"We're free ev'ry day except Saturdays".

The groom, the best man, and bride's father
Ensured that the food in the larder
Was ample and fine,
And likewise the wine –
The cellar stock couldn't be vaster.

Come the day of the great wedding feast
The supply of the wines simply ceased
The M/C and bridegroom
(Aside in the ice room)
Were not in the least bit well pleased.

The Lord and his friends were invited
And soon news of the problem alighted
With that group, and his mother
Told the servants and others
To do just what the Lord indicated.

Those listening to Jesus' commands
Could hardly believe his demands
But they filled the containers
With water – complainers
By the best wine were silenced and charmed.

As time passed, the best man, and the groom
Still wondered what, how, and by whom
Did the strange thing occur -
People politely demurred
But missed the first sign of the Kingdom.

At Capernaum and other parts of Galilee

In Capernaum, Peter's wife's Mum
Had a dreadful bad pain in her tum,
Which, combined with a fever
That just would not leave her,
Made them wonder now what should be done?

But the Lord came and healed her that day,
And at once she got up, cleared away,
And cooked them all dinner –
"What a meal, what a winner,
Praise the Lord" they all said, and "Hooray!"

Healing and the forgiveness of sins

Mark 2: 1-11

There once was a man on a stretcher
Whose friends said, "To Jesus we'll get yer"
And they did – here's the proof –
They demolished the roof
(The reason for which we'll conjecture).

The Lord was stopped short in his tracks:
The man said, "Please help – it's my back
Where I feel all the pain"
"Then don't sin again,"
Said Jesus "You're forgiven, relax!"

The Pharisees stood there and seethed
What they'd heard they could hardly believe
Jesus knew what they thought,
So said "Get up and walk"
Which made them quite furious and peeved.

The Ten Lepers

Ten lepers the Lord healed together
To the temple they went to see whether
The priest would confirm
That the leprosy germ
They'd been freed from would not return ever.

Only one of the lepers came back
Of good manners the nine showed a lack;
But the tenth man demurred
Before thanking the Lord
Who said, 'Good! You are on the right track'.

The Adventure of Bartimaeus

The adventure of blind Bartimaeus
Is a tale to encourage and cheer us,
It was Jesus' last visit
Bart made sure he'd not miss it
By the roadside he sat and called "Jesus".

The rest of the people in Jericho
Snapped "Be Quiet: you don't matter, you know"
But the Lord heard, I dare say,
His cry "Lord have mercy"
And his blindness it vanished, like snow.

Healing on the Sabbath

There once was a man with Erb's palsy
  Whose arms were made worse by the falls he
Sustained – Jesus took him
When the scribes were all looking
In the synagogue where they could all see.

Jesus turned to the scribes, of them asked
"Would healing this man be a task
To avoid on the Sabbath
For which you are gathered?"
They all looked at each other, aghast!

Then he told them, "The Sabbath was given
For you to enjoy – just like heaven,
But you all make rules
Which make you look fools,
Which in turn makes your worship just stiffen".

To the man with the atrophic arm
He said "Stretch – it'll do you no harm
Use it, now it's restored
In the service of God,
Give Him praise – if you like, sing a psalm!

An invalid for 38 years

By a gate in the wall of Jerusalem
There's a pool round which gathered some grueson
Poor wretches deformed
In both body and mind
But folk just walked by – they were used to them.

One man claimed that he'd been there for years
Thirty-eight, in fact, and his worst fears
Confirmed his belief
And compounded his grief,
Where upon he just burst into tears.

Do you want to get better? Jesus said
Or would you rather be tucked up in bed
Now stand up, and pick up
Your mat – just one hiccup
No more "carries", now you walk instead.

A surprise miracle

A blind man they met at Bethsaida
What the Lord did next caused quite a major
Shock and surprise,
Jesus spat in his eyes,
For there seemed to have formed some dyscrasia.

By the second time he laid his hands on
The blind man, his blindness had gone.
Now he could see
Not just people as trees,
But also the Lord – God's dear Son.

Jesus and the madman

A madman possessed so it seems
Was allowed by the kind Gerasenes
To care for their swine
Which helped pass the time -
An offer less good than it seems.

In the graveyard he made his crude home
Where he lived quite entirely alone
When he saw Jesus there
He pulled out his hair
Screaming "keep away – I'm on my own".

"We know" yelled the man, "who you are
And why you have travelled this far
And we are called "Legion"
For we live in this region -
We're so many, we're not sure who we are".

"Don't send us away, we implore you"
The demons balked at the Lord's clear view
"Send us into the swine
And we'll not complain
You scared us from when we first saw you".

The pigs all stampeded as if
They'd all been told "Jump off that cliff"
Neither pigs nor the demon
Survived, but the beam on
The man's face was not to be missed.

Healing for Gentiles, too

A woman from Syro-phonecia
Thought that people would think it beneath her
Correct social standing
To keep on demanding
Her daughter was healed – that would please her.

So she fell down in front of his feet
And begged that the Lord would delete
From her daughter, the demon
Which spoiled lifestyle and reason,
But the Lord seemed aloof and discrete.

She engaged in sharp verbal riposte
Determined her cause was not lost,
Then the Lord showed his power
From that minute, that hour
That young lady was healed – at whose cost?

The story of Jairus' daughter

The story of Jairus' daughter
Began when she asked for more water;
But more water still
Didn't lessen her chill -
Despite her imbibed pint and quarter.

Her condition got rapidly worse
"Get a healer to come" was the terse
Comment made by a neighbour
"This Jesus might save her
I guess its worth trying him first".

Jairus searched for the Lord that same day,
And implored him to come right away
"She's dying, I fear"
He said, wiping a tear
From his face filled with fear and dismay.

And then to the amazement of all
Jesus stopped by a low level wall;
In a voice that was loud
He asked the whole crowd
"Who touched me? Please come when I call".

A woman, who perhaps was embarrassed
Crept forward – she didn't seem harassed
Meanwhile Peter just laughed,
Saying Lord don't be daft
You do say strange things – quite the oddest".

"To touch you fulfilled all my need"
Said the woman knowing well that she'd
Attracted attention
Which was not her intention
From her sickness said Jesus "You're freed".

Meanwhile, back at the household of Jairus
Came the sounds of deep grief – quite the direst
Of loud mournful wailing
That through the village was trailing
A cacophony of wailers called "Hire us".

Into Jairus' home entered Jesus,
With the parents, plus James, John and Peter.
Jesus said "She's not dead –
Feel her pulse, see her head
Wake up, little girl – and now feed her!"

Jesus raises dead people to life: The son of the widow of Nain

There once was a widow of Nain
Whose anguish, sorrow, and pain
All began when her son –
Her beloved number one
Dropped down dead – why? she could not explain

But the Lord, filled with love and compassion,
Stopped the weeping, and wailing, and gnashing
He said "Young man, arise,
Wake up, open your eyes" -
Which he did in a most lively fashion.

Lazarus

Of dear Lazarus we're told, he was sick
Then he died, we are told, pretty quick
Jesus said, "From this story
They'll give God the glory
Once they see it's for real – and no trick".

When Jesus arrived, they were thinking
Lazarus' body must really be stinking
Jesus went to the tomb
Shouted into the gloom -
Some thought that he must have been drinking.

Very soon came the sound of a shuffle
And a voice that was muted by muffle;
"I feel really funny
Dressed up like a mummy -
Get me out please, or soon I'll be stifled".

With what ecstasy Lazarus came home!
He'd been freed from the bonds of the tomb,
He looked very well
Not a vestige of smell -
Not a stain on his white dressing-gown.

At home they'd prepared lots of food
For the mourners, of whom some were rude
So the sisters of Lazarus
Said "Hey, give that to us"
The mourners were sent home and booed!

Now some of the crowd were quite sceptical,
"All he needed", they said, "was a receptacle
Containing a fragrance
Such as cures fainting maidens –
It's doubtful that Lazarus was dead at all".

For the most part they agreed that he'd died;
That the cool of the tomb had revived
Him was plainly untrue,
But some plotters withdrew
To plan their solution – homicide.

But Caiaphas was that year's high priest;
And said to the people "At least
The truth now is dawning:
Forthwith cease your mourning;
Let one man alone be deceased.

But the greatest of miracles ever
Is that we shall be saved altogether
"Jesus Lives" is the reason
Death's no longer a prison;
All heaven sings "Praise God" and "How clever!"

The Biggest Picnic Ever

One day the Lord preached a long sermon
So late was the hour, dusk was falling
The Lord asked the lads "How
This hungry tired crowd
Would survive if there was no food for them?"

A young lad slid closely to Andrew
And asked "Anything that I can do?
I'll give you my lunch …"
Andrew then had a hunch
That the Lord knew what's coming – a grand do!

Thus the world's biggest picnic began
With five rolls and two fish, but no jam
Five thousand at least
Had a spiritual feast
But no turkey, no beef, nor fresh lamb.

Giving thanks, Jesus blessed all the food
It all looked so wholesome and good
This picnic was shared
No-one need've despaired
For each person consumed all they could

When the picnic would soon be complete
And folk's sandals were back on their feet
Jesus said "Leave it tidy
Today is a Friday
Ensure that we leave it all neat".

Adventures in a boat

The disciples got caught in a squall
Which scared them to bits one and all
What frightened them most
(They thought was a ghost)
Was Jesus not sinking at all.

The Lord appeared walking on water
Simon Peter tried. Failed. "Did you oughter?"
Said the Lord, "Now think why?
Should you e'en want to try
Peter sank as he started to falter.

But the Lord quickly came to his rescue
He said "Simon, I needed to test you
Will you still follow me
Absolutely, fault-free?"
Said Peter "That's why we've not left you".

On another occasion, at sea
In the stern of the small boat was he
Sound asleep, unaware
Of the danger they feared,
For the angry storm filled Galilee.

Jesus yawned and woke up gently thinking
The disciples said "Quick, Lord, we're sinking
But the Lord opened wide
Both his arms and his eyes
And commanded the storm to cease, winking.

What kind of a man is this Jesus?
The disciples, amongst themselves, pleaded
The winds and the weather
Obey him whatever
This world must soon realise he's needed.

One-to-ones with Jesus: Zacchaeus

The collection of taxes in Jericho
Was all done by Zacchaeus, as most know,
His gross overcharging
Gave a huge profit margin
And the loss of his friends who he used to know.

Zacchaeus developed a notion
That he'd rather not cause a commotion;
For though he was short
His small bone-frame had taught
Him to climb trees with minimal motion.

At the foot of the sycamore tree
Jesus stopped, smiled, and looked up to see
If this man had absconded
Or better, responded
To what, if he wanted, could be.

Jesus called up the tree to Zacchaeus
"Are you coming on down now to see us?"
With embarrassing glee
Zacchaeus invited to tea
All the people he'd wronged. How mysterious!

Nicodemus

There once was a teacher supremus
Whose friends called him "Our Nicodemus"
He arranged an appointment,
For he had an assortment
Of queries he wished to ask Jesus.

Jesus told him "You must be reborn"
He replied, feeling rather forlorn
"How can you replace
Back in-utero space
That which through birth has life of its own?"

Rebirth with both water and Spirit
Is the way that the good Lord would have it
For to enter the kingdom
Of heaven be like children
Drink his love for your thirst – he'll instil it.

For God loved the world, Jesus said
That he let his dear Son come. Instead
Of allowing each person –
From the best to the worst one
To die, for all Christ's blood was shed.

The woman at the well

At Sychar there is an old well
Dating back many years – Israel
Gave it to his son Joseph
But nobody knows if
It has any stories to tell.

On a walk by the well, Jesus rested
A Samaritan woman suggested
That she'd get him a drink
Though the neighbours might think
"Aren't the Jews in Samaria detested?"

Jesus answered "If only you knew
God's great gift, and who stands before you,
Then you'd ask me first
To quench your great thirst
With a spiritual spring – that I'd do".

The rich young man

There was a young man who asked Jesus
"What personal cost would be needed
To acquire life eternal
Free from all things infernal?"
Jesus looked at the man, who acceded.

Then the Lord taught the crowd about riches
"It's the love and excess of them which is
The way to disaster
For when wealth is your master
The desire for possession makes hitches".

Simon of Bethany, and the woman who interrupted the dinner party

During supper with Simon of Bethany
A woman came forward, and asked if she
Could anoint Jesus' feet
With pure oil exquisite
The guests were amazed – Jesus let her be.

She knelt before Jesus in tears
And kissed his feet gently with care
The folk standing around said
"We're really astounded…"
"It's not" Jesus said, "as appears".

"What a waste", said young Judas Iscariot
"It would have been better to sell the lot
And give to the poor
Who sit outside your door
(After that against Jesus he plots).

Jesus looked at his host, who looked sad,
"Does what has occurred make you glad?
Or embarrassed or angry?"
Jesus asked the proud Pharisee
And a few awkward moments were had.

Jesus turned to the woman, and said
"Your sins are forgiven, instead
Of your present sad lifestyle
Which you've followed for some while
You've a brand new perspective ahead".

Then to Simon he turned and complained
"When I got here, you never explained
Why you showed me no courtesies
That etiquette says should be
Offered to guests and to friends.

But this woman was desperate to rid
Herself from the things that she did
Her gratitude's greater
And God will remake her
And record for all time "How Splendid".

The Stories of Jesus

Jesus spoke to the people in story -
Gave them just a quick glimpse of God's glory
Much sickness he healed,
And the gospel appealed
To all who were hampered by worry.

To the twelve he revealed a bit more -
How he came to fulfil all "The Law",
And the "Prophets" as well
For they all of them tell
Of God's kingdom that'll last evermore.

The Sower

There once was a sower out sowing
On a day when the wind, it was blowing:
Some seed fell on the path,
Which made the birds laugh,
And some where the thorns stopped it growing.

But most ended up in the field,
Where it gave a quite excellent yield
That's the end of the story
I don't want to bore you,"
Said Jesus, his listeners just smiled.

Two Builders

On a rock did the wise fellow build
His new house – its foundations were filled
With the best shale and gravel
Rolled and crushed till quite level
Thus the house weathered storms fierce and wild.

But the stupid and lazy contractor
Built large houses that definitely lacked a
Foundation – his land
Comprised nearly all sand,
Which angered the Buildings Inspector.

The Hidden Treasure

A man who was digging at leisure
In a field found a chest full of treasure
He sold all else he had
(All his friends thought him mad)
Bought the field – he was rich beyond measure.

Yeast

The kingdom of heaven's like yeast
Which was kneaded for bread at a feast
The yeast permeated
The people who ate it
From the greatest one there to the least.

The Invitation

The kingdom is like an occasion
Attendance is by invitation
The invites all stress
That the right sort of dress
Is compulsory – no variation.

The fate of Dives

There once was a rich man called Dives
Who disdained all the poor, asking "Why these
Dregs of society
Must always bother me"
But that night they all had surprises.

For during the night they all died
When they woke, they were on diff'rent sides
Of a vast dark ravine
With no way in between
The poor were now blest, the rich cried.

The Good Samaritan

A man was out walking to Jericho
But got mugged and attacked by a weirdo;
He was badly assaulted –
His features distorted
All the mugger would say was, "Well there you go!"

Very soon a smart Anglican vicar
Passing by, said, "It would be much quicker
If I went to get help
So don't move, shout, or whelp",
But the victim got sicker much quicker.

Then a social work expert, walked by,
Took a look, and then said, "I know why
This assault has occurred –
The poor man is a nerd!
'Tis for therapy we should apply".

Now the third passer-by was a dealer
In second hand cars and three wheelers
When he saw the man's state
He said, "Come on my mate,
I'll take you to someone 'ool 'eal yer".

So he took him straight down to the pub,
Found the landlord, said "Get 'im some grub
For this poor bashed up fellow's
All shades of yellow
And 'ere is some liniment rub".

"An' finally, 'ere's fifty quid
If that i'n't enough, – my name's Sid
What ever 'e's needing –
Be it medicines or feeding
Then do let 'im 'ave it, Eh kid?"

The Lost Sheep

There once was a sheep that got lost,
But his shepherd, discounting the cost
Searched the land till he'd found him,
Put a safe fence around him,
And with all of his friends, he rejoiced.

The Lost Coin

A woman who lost a small coin
Swept her house out, making sure that the nine
Other coins of pure silver
Were safe and were still where
She'd put them – "They're there, good that's fine".

But the lost coin herself she had found,
All her neighbours she invited, "Come round
Have a nice cup of tea,
And praise God with me,
Now I've found it, I've no cause to frown!"

The Lost Sons

The son, known through history as "Prodigal"
Was both rude and so mean and methodical
His own father he conned
Out of cash, deeds, and bonds,
Which he spent at a speed quite incredible.

Very soon all the fortune had gone -
He left nothing which once had belonged
to his generous old Dad,
Whose friends thought he was mad
When he said he'd forgive the lad's wrongs.

But one day the lad did return
And realised he'd no need to earn
His father's forgiveness
He lavished his goodness
Which was far greater than he could discern.

The point of these three tales of losers
Is to show how all heaven rejoices
When those who are sinners
Repent so they're winners,
For God loves all those whom he chooses.

Two Men in the Temple

Two men went to church to say prayers:
One posh guy, all full of his airs
And graces said "Lord
You must get so bored
When the simple folk greet you with "Cheers!"

The other guy, jeans all in tatters,
Said, "God, I don't know if it matters,
I've been bad and I've messed
Up my life – it's no jest:
Can you mend it? It's what you'd call shattered.

The pompous and priggish old chappie
Then came out of the church so they all could see
How holy he looked -
And how notably hooked
He was with his flagrant narcissity.

The other guy slipped out at the side
Of the church where it wasn't too wide
He hoped no-one would see
Yet his life now felt free
And forgiven, right through, and inside.

The Talents

There once was a man whose estate
With ease cut into pieces of eight
He called his three servants
Said "Make sure you've learnt that
I expect that a fortune, you'll make".

Then he called his three servants in turn
So that they would quite quickly discern
His sole interest was profit
A loss would just not fit
He'd settle up on his return.

To the first, gave five talents – the most
"Just to make money, not boast"
To the second he gave two
Said "That's quite enough for you"
To the third he gave one – the lowest.

He came back many years later
Two servants reported the state of
His wealth – it had doubled
But the third one was troubled
For fear that they'd call him a traitor.

The rich man was angry and mad
"If you'd banked it, it wouldn't be bad
But stuck in a pot
And buried to rot –
Give it back faithless servant – you're sad.

The unforgiving debtor

There once was a man who owed money
But considered repayments quite funny
When his Visa exceeded
Its limit, he pleaded
With the credit controller "Hey, Sonny.

"Just lend me a few thousand more?"
The controller just showed him the door
"Unless you repay
What the rule books all say
We'll bankrupt you under the law".

But the man duly pleaded his case
To be let off the debt – the disgrace
Of being made bankrupt
Would for ever disrupt
His street cred – he'd have egg on his face.

So the credit man said, "That's Okay,
It's my birthday – we'll think of a way
To write off your debt
It's the biggest one yet!
Let's make it a real happy day"

Now a colleague at work had said "I've
A small cashflow shortfall, lend me five
I'll repay you next week,
But I'd rather not speak
Of just why I need this to survive".

The first man with haste left the room
Found his colleague – snarled "Pay me back soon –
I want that cash now,
And I do not care how
You get it, from where, or from whom".

The credit controller was curious;
When he heard the whole tale, he was furious;
"I shall cancel his rating
Without any waiting
So far as I care, he is spurious".

Wheat and Weeds

A farmer who seeded his fields
With the best crop of corn-seed that yields
The highest return
Was appalled when he learned
That the fields were all spoiled by large weeds.

"Who ever has made all this mess?"
Asked his servants, "An enemy, I guess
Has deliberately spoiled
Where we all have toiled
In an effort to make us depressed.

Cheer up – you all look so forlorn
Let the weeds grow in with the corn
And when it is harvest
The task that'll be hardest
Will be burning the tares – not the corn."

The Tale of the Goats and the Sheep

The tale of the goats and the sheep
(like the tale of the five maids, asleep)
Warns 'gainst spiritual slumber
(And of being hungover)
But awake and alert we should keep.

The three synoptic gospels say much
About "Apocalyptic" and such.
The end of the world
Has been often foretold
But some people are scared, and won't touch.

The story of the wicked tenants

There once was a grower of vines
Who produced the most beautiful wines
He went off on a voyage
Leaving farmhands in charge
While he went round the world several times.

When the time came to taste what fermented
The farmhands thought hard, and invented
A great mass of lies
Which was a surprise
As he'd thought they were loyal and contented.

So he sent his dear Son to collect
What he hoped was the bestest wine yet
But the farmhands planned murder;
Which the owner soon heard of
And the tenants were thrown out direct.

The sayings and teachings of Jesus

Is it right to pay tribute to Caesar"
Was a question the scribes thought would please a
Lot of the Jews
Who disliked paying dues -
"So tell us the answer please Jesus!"

Jesus asked to see one of the coins
And asked them to tell him who owns
The inscription and writing -
(though it's not very exciting,
And extracted a chorus of groans).

Reluctant, they muttered "It's Caesar's"
"Then give to the emperor", said Jesus,
"The things that are his
And to God, who still gives
Us such good things, sing gladly his praises".

When a guest at a banquet or party,
Keep your profile low – don't be too hearty;
Pay attention to manners,
Never wave your own banners,
And your host will declare, "Here's a smartie!"

For the person who seeks to be greater
Will for certain end up as the waiter
For the last shall be first,
And the first (at the worst) -
Their come-uppance will catch them up later.

The man with a beam in his eye
Is a fool if (though clumsy) he tries
To remove a small sliver
Of wood from another
Whilst retaining the beam in his eye.

"When you're praying to God, say 'Our Father'
For that is the way that he'd rather
His children addressed him
And then he can bless them;
Its straight talking he wants, not palaver.

Seek the Lord, and for certain you'll find
That He's merciful, loving, and kind;
A God of pure justice,
In whose confidence our trust is
Eternal, secure, and refined.

"Seek the Kingdom of God first", he said,
"It's God's stated intention to spread
His sweet song of salvation
To each tribe and nation -
Let them all hear the gospel" he read.

Let the light of Christ's love shine through you
That all people can see what you do
And the skills you've acquired
(Which your friends have admired)
Will draw them to Jesus Christ too.

Let your light shine like lamps on a hill
That keep on and on burning, until
They are known as a landmark
Ever present when it's dark
Shining on in both rough winds and still.

The rich, Jesus warned, find it hard
To enter God's kingdom unscarred;
They can't buy their way in,
Only pardon from sin
Is the sure way to faith in the Lord.

The sartorial excellence of Solomon
Has been copied for centuries long
But the gorgeous white lily —
Clothed so simply – not frilly
Is a far better vestment – c'est bon.

Meditation will not make hair grow
Nor can height be achieved quick or slow
So why do you worry
And race round in a hurry?
All your needs does your Father God know.

The Beatitudes

Blessed" said Jesus, "are those
Who are poor in the spirit, God knows
For the kingdom is theirs
They are God's rightful heirs
For they are the ones that God chose".

"Blessed, too are the people who mourn
No longer shall they stay forlorn
But real spiritual comfort
Just like a clear trumpet
Will restore to them joy, come the morn".

"Blessed also", he said, "Are the meek
Likewise those who diligently seek
For the qualities found in
The kingdom of heaven
Such as turning the opposite cheek".

"Blessed are those with a thirst
That the kingdom of God should come first
For their hunger in reaching
Lost souls – they'll be preaching
The Gospel – The Good News that works".

"Blessed, too, are all those who show mercy
When it seems that men try hard to
Persecute you for the sake
Of the gospel, then take
Courage, rejoice, it could worse be!".

"Blessed, next, are those who are pure
To see God is their promise secure
Blessed those who seek peace
Both the great and the least
That they'll be in the kingdom's for sure".

"Blessed are those who are martyrs
Or prisoners of conscience for starters
Because of your faith
The church honours your place
Both in this life, and in the hereafter".

"Blessed are you if in trouble
For the sake of the gospel… don't muddle
The vagaries of man
With the devil's crude plans -
Your reward up in heaven will be double".

The I AM's of John

The way that the story is told
In John's gospel, is designed to uphold
The truths of the text
And you never know next
What might happen as the story unfolds.

There are seven claims by Jesus, that he
Is the Lord of the earth, sky and sea
Each starts with "I AM" Son of God, Son of Man?
God's own lamb, yes that's what it's to be..

First of all "I'm the true bread of life
(Not the type that you cut with a knife)
I'm the bread that's from heaven
For my body is given
For you to protect you from strife".

"I am the light of the world
Despite all the insults they hurled
At me for showing
The way that you're going
And that by my love you're enfurled".

"I am the door, (or the gate)
I know you so well, like a mate
Each sheep knows my voice
Each sheep's mine by choice
And remains mine for ever – that's great!"

"I am also the shepherd, who's good
I'll defend all the sheep as I should
There's no price too high
That this shepherd won't pay
Even death – with the shedding of blood".

"I am the resurrection life
Those who trust me, despite earthly strife
Life eternal shall see
God alone shall for me
Promise goodness where love can run rife".

"I am the way and the truth
And the life, and here is the proof
I'm the way to the Father –
There is simply no other
For never will I stand aloof".

"I am the one holy vine
Into me you are grafted – that's fine
But the more that whatever
Moves us closer together
The better the fruit and the wine".

The Transfiguration

Up the mountain of transfiguration
The Lord took three friends one occasion
The two sons of thunder
Like Peter, did wonder
What next would need clear explanation.

In a moment or two, a vast cloud
Which had covered them, broke, and a loud
Clear voice spoke – its for real
Not a joke – so please kneel
Its my son of whom I'm justly proud.

Then a vision of Moses and Elijah
Who talked with the Lord right beside where
The three friends sat down
Overcome by renown
Blurted Peter "Let's build tents, and abide here".

Back to Reality

By the time they'd come down from the mount
They were tired almost out for the count
Jesus asked just one question
"Who am I – what suggestions?"
Peter said "The Messiah – there's no doubt".

To make all the teaching more relevant
And remembered with skill, like the elephant
The Lord told short stories;
But in the end more is
Retained if you see the event.

Therefore miracles he did so's to teach them
That God's love for ever will reach them
So when you proclaim
That you speak in his name
Take the sayings of Jesus, and preach them.

The Lord had a soft spot for children
"Of such is the kingdom of heaven
And unless you accept it
There's no chance you'll get it
For that's what the Father has given".

The final journey

The time came for the Lord's final journey
To Jerusalem, sat on a donkey
The crowd cried "Hosanna"
And waved palms and banners
A week later the same crowd was surly.

The next day he went to the temple
Where leaders set such poor examples
Resembling a market,
Inside notice how dark it
Was spiritually as well as temporal.

The Lord's anger exploded – he drove
The loan sharks bright red, then to mauve.
He said "Don't you grouse
This is my Father's house
Any not here for worship – out goes".

The Passion Story: The Last Supper

In the midst of the "Passover" rituals
Jesus told his disciples, "These victuals
Will now take on new meaning -
You'll learn more this evening
When I shall rejoice to be with you all".

"For bread is my body that's broken
Eat it often, for it is a token
Of a joyful new era
When these things will seem clearer
And God's purpose to all will be open".

The choicest best wine was outpoured
The cup was shared round by the Lord
The stunned guests were silent
A deep sense of discontent
Ran eerily through each and all.

Jesus took a clean towel and some water
And washed each man's feet – You all ought to
Wash each other's feet
Without flinch, without bleat
For that is the way you've been taught to.

But Peter protested his need
"I'm not worthy", he spluttered, "indeed
'Tis I should be washing
Your feet, and you splashing
Both the inside and outside of me".

The Last Covenant

He then spoke of the kingdom of heaven,
Of God's love, and of sins now forgiven,
But the prayers of the Lord
In John's gospel are stored,
And the anguish with which He was riven.

After supper they went for a walk.
Part in silence, then Jesus would talk
Of the heavenly home
He'd prepare for his own
A dwelling-place where they'd not balk.

On reaching the garden Gethsemane
Jesus asked his disciples "Please pray with me"
But their spirits were dreary
Their eyelids too weary
Thus the Lord sat awaiting his enemy.

Jesus is arrested

A mob captured him out in the garden,
Judas' heart had now started to harden,
And Malchus' ear
Peter made disappear
(Which earned a reproof and a pardon).

(The swift severance of Malchus' ear
Was effected by sword – that's quite clear,
But revasculisation
Without hesitation
Healed at once, and ensured he could hear.)

The disciples followed on at a distance
Driven on by an inner insistence
That they should obey
Jesus Christ all the way –
But they made no attempt at resistance.

He was brought before the High Priest
Who was up there because of the feast;
People said He'd blasphemed
(So they claimed it had seemed)
And all semblance of truth had long ceased.

Simon Peter kept distance outside
Of the courtyard – he tried hard to hide
But he'd heard the cock crow
And at once tried to go
But the Lord looked at Peter, who cried.

At the trial of the Lord, Peter blew it
Asked if he knew "This Jesus", he withdrew a bit
Then with language appalling
He heard the cock calling
And the Lord looked at Peter, who knew it.

In the end the crowd screamed "He must die"
Then to Pilate they yelled "Crucify
Him now, don't refuse
Your loyal people, the Jews",
Which inspired Pilate's feeble "But why?"

The rest of the trial was a farce -
Between Pilate and Herod he passed;
In the end they assailed Him,
To rough wood they nailed him,
Shouting verbal abuse to the last.

With two bandits the Lord was to die;
"It is finished!" His ultimate cry,
They took His corpse down
Removing the crown
Of thorns, bitterly asking God "Why?"

The Burial - the Resurrection of Jesus Christ

Now young Joseph of Arimathea
Had a tomb that was empty and clear;
To the Lord he did lend
It for the weekend
Knowing really there's nothing to fear.

On Day three, from the dead Christ arose
The cross had been God's coup de grace
The stone rolled away
Was the proof of the day
When death was defeated at last.

The Appearances by Jesus after the Resurrection

The reinstatement by Jesus of Peter
Was a matter so brief he'd no need to
Be the least apprehensive
Or anxious, or pensive:
All the Lord asked to know was much sweeter.

"Simon, Jonas's son, do you love me?"
Jesus asked "Lord, you know that I love thee"
Was Peter's reply
Though he couldn't think "why
Such a strange little thing did he ask me".

As they walked along that well known shore
Jesus posed the same question twice more
Peter's quiet irritation
Matched his slight hesitation
Just what had he let himself in for?

On the third day when Peter went fishing
So remorseful and desperately wishing
That he'd rescued the Lord
Then escaped through the crowd
In a rather brave "Pimpernel" fashion.

Peter thought of the women who'd gone
To the tomb, barely had the dawn come,
How they'd met with an angel
Who told them "Be sure and tell
Peter I'm risen – we've won!"

With young John he'd been down to the tomb
Very early, and peered through the gloom
He remembered that he must be
Heading for Galilee
Hoping to meet the Lord soon.

But then filled with gloom and remorse
He'd gone out night fishing, and of course
His catch came to zero
If only his hero
Were here, Peter longed for his voice.

The walk to Emmaus
(and back again)

Two friends on their way to Emmaus
Were discussing "the things that dismay us"
They were joined by a third
Who seemed not to have heard
Of "the things that then seemed to amaze us".

When they got to their planned destination
They succeeded by gentle persuasion
To invite him to join
Them in bread and some wine
Which he took, blessed, and broke, and then gave them.

Then he disappeared out of their sight
But by now they knew, with delight
That their eyes had been opened
Clouds of doubt had been broken
This was Jesus the Lord of great might.

The Lord appeared to them all (except Thomas)

When the Lord first appeared, the disciples
Were all in one place, except Thomas
Who missed this encounter
And started to wonder
If the others had dumped all their scruples.

"It's just wishful thinking" he said
"We all know that Jesus is dead
So unless I can touch
His hands, wrist, and side... Such
Proof is vital to clear out my head."

One week later the Lord reappeared.
The disciples were jubilant, and cheered
Jesus turned straight to Thomas
And said "Look at me – not as
The world does – they've always just jeered."

The once-sceptic Thomas now knew
There was only one thing he could do
(Though in some ways quite hard)
Cried "My Lord and my God!"
Jesus answered "You know now it's true."

He appeared to his friends quite a lot -
Made them query the body he'd got;
For just when He was there
He'd gone into thin air;
"Was He here", they would ask, "Was He not?"

The Ascension

The last time He appeared was "Ascension",
About which he'd made little mention;
He went up in a cloud,
And the small select crowd
Wondered just what had been his intention.

Then two angels asked, "Why are you here?
Can't you see – He is really not there
But one day he'll return
And to all will affirm
That He's King and He's Lord everywhere".

Meanwhile, off to Jerusalem go,
And at Pentecost, then you will know
What the Spirit can do
With a weird bunch like you
In response the disciples said, "Oh!"

A replacement for Judas was sought
Two names, both quite worthy were brought;
When they voted, Matthias
Scored easily the highest
Then on as "Apostle" he taught.

Pentecost - The Church is born

The Spirit at Pentecost came
And Baptised the disciples with flame
By wind, tongues of fire
Everyone was inspired
The GOOD NEWS then to boldly proclaim.

In Jerusalem, Jews from each nation
Had met in divine convocation
It amazed everyone
That their own native tongue
Was spoken in clear explanation.

The Parthians, Jews and the Medes
Found they had quite differing creeds
Whilst from Mesopotamia
They wondered "Why came we here?
Or is this the way that God leads?"

Egyptians, and Cretians, and Arabs
Witnessed things even greater than "Harrods"
But the folk from Judea
And Cappodocia
Ran around like excited young scarabs.

There grew an increasing loud hubbub
Which caused Simon Peter to stand up
And explain to the crowd
In a voice clear and loud
What had happened, and what would be set up.

Peter chided the crowd – "Drunk we're not
See the sundial – it's before nine o'clock
But if you've read Joel
No doubt you will know all
The promises God made – there's a lot.

For God will pour out his Spirit
On everyone who will receive it,
And each person who called
On the name of the Lord
Was released from their sin – God just did it!

Tales from the Acts

The young Church in Action's" a thriller,
And St Luke could quite easily fill a
Few more editions
And several revisions
That would soon occupy a large cellar.

Very soon it was obvious they'd need a
Gifted person to act as a leader
The choice of them all
Was in fact not St Paul,
But unquestionably that of St Peter.

Peter and John, one fine day
Went up to the temple to pray
It was just three o'clock –
They had a mild shock
When a beggar said "You'll have to pay"

Said John "We're deficient in cash
And round here all they deal in is trash
But we've got something better –
Stand up, and you'll get a
Surprise – you will walk, jump, and dash

There once was a wizard called Simon
Who certainly was not a sly man
He offered straight cash
In exchange for panache
Thinking "that's a good number I'll be on".

Simon Peter's response was of anger;
The wizard saw he'd dropped a clanger
Of massive proportions
Much wider than oceans
In sorrow he knelt as a sinner.

A man who was called Ananias
Sold some land off, but gave away less
Than what he said that he'd got
For the sale of the plot
Such behaviour was not very nice.

Peter quickly saw through the sad man
To boost his own ego his plan
But when challenged by Peter
He wobbled and teetered
And collapsed in a heap on the sand.

Three hours later, Sapphira returned
Of her husband's death she'd not yet learned
Peter told her the story
"He's dead white and hoary"
He said. Then Sapphira expired.

The reason this tale is included
Is because many folk are deluded
Into not thinking why
Jesus Christ came to die
Research shows in fact very few did...

Simon Peter had been roughly arrested
Even though many Christians protested
But angelic release
Got him free then at least
To make his own way unmolested.

When he got to the door of the house
All was quiet as th'proverbial church mouse
And he knocked very hard
On the door to the yard
Till someone at last was aroused.

A servant girl, known just as Rhoda
Wouldn't open the door till they'd showed her
That the voice in the night
Was dear Peter's alright
(Twas his looks and his voice – not his odour).

Stephen - The First Martyr

There was a young deacon called Stephen
Who, one day, had a vast crowd believing
That Jesus had died -
For all people – world wide
So great was his powerful preaching.

He was lucid in argument, too
All the synagogue leaders soon knew
They admitted that "No-one does
Great signs and wonders as
Graciously, Stephen as you".

A small group of Jewish extremists
Conspired against Stephen. Their remits
Were to wreck and disgrace him
Then they'd not have to face him
And his character? none would redeem it.

They connived with some men to tell lies
And insisted there'd been blasphemies
They said, "There has got to be
Fraud and apostasy,
Therefore", they said, "Stephen dies".

So they set up a counterfeit court
Charged and sentenced him without a thought
Then killed him by stoning
Completely disowning
What they'd done just was not what they ought.

The Man from Ethiopia

An ambassador from Ethiopia
Spent his spare time in search of Utopia;
He was keen to acquire
The book of Isaiah
And whilst reading it, got very much closer.

The Spirit led Philip the deacon
To ask if he knew what the meaning
Of what he had read
Still remained in his head,
Or whether he'd carry on seeking.

So keen was the eunuch to find
The meaning, he just didn't mind
That the deacon explained
Every detail contained
In the law and the prophets combined.

At last deacon Philip surmised
What the Eunuch desired "Please baptise
Me – here's water
Do it now, please don't falter
But the eunuch was in for a surprise".

For as they climbed out of the lake,
The eunuch asked "Am I awake?"
For he could hardly believe
What the preacher achieved:
Philip vanished from sight – no mistake.

In fact he was seen back in Azortus -
The story he told will have taught us
To pray in the Spirit
Keep on to the limit
And remember your sons and your daughters.

Saul becomes Paul:
the persecutor becomes the apostle

A zealous young Pharisee called Saul
Was involved and part of it all
He'd consented to murder –
On the grape vine he'd heard a
Conspiracy to kill, kill them all.

"Them all" referred to "The Way",
A nickname that had, so they say
Been given to Christians
(And written by historians)
In a most appropriate way.

On the road to Damascus, young Saul
Was then stopped in his tracks by the call
Of the Lord asking "Why
Do you persecute my
Friends with such anger and gall?"

By the brilliant white light he was blinded
And at once asked his friends if they minded
Holding hands as they walked
(But none of them talked)
What it meant – they were all undecided.

His travelling companions declined
To believe he'd be permanently blind
So this zealot from Tarsus
Was led to Damascus
In the hope that his sight he would find.

A godly man called Ananias
Had a vision: God said "Have no bias
For this reprobate Saul
Is the man I shall call
To carry my name to the Gentiles.

With caution and great apprehension,
The Christian disciples made mention
Of Saul's militant aim
To destroy the Lord's name
Which till now was his stated intention.

None the less they received him in love
He acknowledged the God that's above
Then scales fell from his eyes
He at once was baptised –
By the Lord he'd been totally reproved.

There's no doubt the conversion of Saul
Had a dramatic effect upon all
Of matters contemporary
That have shaped history –
The impact was not at all small.

The name change from "Saul" into "Paul"
Seemed to happen with no fuss at all;
Whilst King Saul, tall and handsome
Would make a fine ransom
The Apostle was wiry and small.

Simon Peter's Vision

In the town Herod named Caesarea
Lived Cornelius a great man of prayer;
In an afternoon vision
He had faced a decision
"Go to Joppa – Simon Peter waits there".

Meanwhile Simon was up on the roof
Receiving a gentle reproof
For he had declined
To eat food unrefined;
From the food he was shown, stood aloof.

Peter looked at the menu three times
"Help yourself" said the Lord, "taste the wines
It is all 'Cordon Bleu'"
Replied Peter "Mon Dieu"
And it's garnished with best "Les herbs fines".

Then abruptly the vision just faded
For a moment the apostle looked jaded
Then, briskly to Caesarea
Met with Cornelius there
And the "Good News" of Jesus paraded!

Cornelius then was baptised
In a manner the Spirit devised
Yet still Simon Peter -
(Not now fetish eater)
Remained by the vision surprised.

Paul's Vision

In Troas St.Paul had a vision
Of a man full of skill and precision
'Please visit us soon –
Before the next moon"
Was his simple and humble petition.

Paul and Silas made haste to get ready
Though excited they kept themselves steady
But meanwhile dear Lydia
Found herself getting giddier
A happy and born-again lady.

The market place in Macedonia
Was the centre of where all the trades-folk are
Here they met a slave-girl –
A "Give-you-a-wave" girl
Bewitched by the men who claimed owning her.

With authority Paul called the demon
To leave the young lass free from "He-men"
Her employers were curious,
Then became furious
Paul and Silas were taken to prison

At midnight at Phillipi prison
Paul and Silas were both awake singing
They'd both been arrested
Pushed about and molested
But they stuck to their song "Christ is risen".

It was dark, then a piercing bright light
Was followed by tremor – which fright-
-ened the others –
the pushers and shuvvers
Who were mesmerised for the whole night.

The governor was scared that the 'quake
Would let all of the prisoners escape
Which meant curtains for him
But Paul stopped him in time
'Else for certain his own life he'd take.

The governor's first question to Paul
Was "What can I do for them all?"
My family, The prisoners
Said Paul "It's my business
To teach you "Believe in the Lord".

For God has promised new life
To those who are hampered by strife
Let the Spirit revive you
Come, let us Baptise you
Your household, your children, your wife.

When speaking of Paul's brilliant distich
Peter asked his friends did they know which is
The greatest commandment
They replied, with discernment
For fear they'd make a grave mistitch.

The question of Paul's vast theology
(See Galatians, sixth chapter, verse twenty-three)
Was down to hard study
Keeping brain clear, not muddy
And a close walk with God in great unity.

Eutychus

Now St Paul was a notable preacher,
And pastor, and writer, and teacher,
But his sermons were boring,
And caused some loud snoring
Which was quite an unfortunate feature.

There was a young man, named Eutychus
Who fell out of a window – Oh what a fuss
He fell on to his head
His friends thought he was dead
They mourned greatly his death – "He was one of us".

His fall was from the third story
He'd been listening to Paul's detailed theory
When he dropped off to sleep
No-one nudged him to keep
Wide awake, though the sermon was dreary.

The apostle was quite unperturbed
He laid the lad flat, and demurred
For a moment, then prayed
All his friends were amazed
For the young man was quite undisturbed.

By the next day he was fully recovered
The apostle felt sure he'd discovered
That the breaking of bread
(Just as the Lord said)
Was a token of all Christ had suffered.

Paul's missionary journeys

Paul's missionary trips round the 'Med'
Were exactly just what he had said
The spread of God's grace
Was explained in each place
And the synagogue leaders turned red.

At some towns a new church was founded
And then the whole gospel resounded
But when gross opposition
Disrupted each mission
Then outside of that town they'd be hounded.

The last that we hear, Paul's in Rome
Where he'd made a new temporary home
He'd appealed to see Caesar
Since at birth he'd achieved a
Citizenship entirely his own.

Paul the persecuted

Many times St Paul landed in prison
His crime? Preaching Jesus was risen
But the more he was taunted
The less he was daunted
And prayed for his foes 'You're forgiven'.

St Paul had a narrow escape
In a basket, concealed by a drape
His friends lowered him down
The outer wall of the town
All his foes did was stand there and gape.

The letters to the young churches

Before writing to any young church
St Paul made a detailed research
Of that which they needed -
Then with God interceded,
To ensure they weren't left in the lurch.

"It's in Romans", declared Martin Luther
"That you can discover the truth
about justification
Through faith, not oblation,
Chapter five will produce all the proof".

To the Christians at Corinth, Paul wrote
At least twice – the words stuck in his throat
But the church was so cluttered by
Gossip that fluttered by -
The gospel had virtually no hope.

Yet despite all their faults, Paul gave thanks
Whenever he heard of those saints
Who were true to the gospel
No matter just what style
Of meeting place they might frequent.

One Corinthians, chapter thirteen
Is a portion of scripture that's been
First choice as a reading
At many a wedding
The best accolade that's been seen.

None the less the Corinthians were told
Of the mysteries that Jesus foretold
And the certain return
Of the Lord made them burn
With new love where it once had been cold.

St. Paul's final command to these people
Was to follow God's ways – not be feeble;
And to heed his appeal,
Follow peace that was real
And serve each the other as equals.

The Christians who lived in Galatia
Suffered badly from spiritual malacia
They rejected "Adoption"
Preferring the Option
Of safety in legal regalia.

"O you foolish Galatians" said P
"You'll end up with no freedom – you'll see
Who has tricked you – not faith,
Which was given you by grace
It's for freedom that Christ set you free".

The church that arose from the Ephesians
Found they'd enemies keen to get even
All the dark powers of evil
Aimed for total upheaval
And collapse of all good – that's the reason.

But the wise wear the armour of God
The protection it gives makes it hard
For the prince of the dark
To inflict any mark
On the soldier of Christ who has dared.

The saints of Christ Jesus in Philippi
Were renowned for their warm generosity
The hymn of Christ's nature
Served well as a feature:
Even so they were short on church unity.

The church was well established at Colossae
Thus Paul gave a lecture on what he
Considered essential
In terms penitential
Including just how we all came to be.

The two letters to Thessalonica
Are both taken up with what might occur
When the Lord in his glory
Rounds off the great story ..
His return is for real – that's certain sure.

The brethren at Laodicea
Were recorded as faithful, that's clear
But one gets the impression
That lack of transgression
Made them dull and unlikely to cheer.

The letters Paul wrote to young Tim
Were specifically written to him,
Whilst the letter to Titus
Was more ubiquitous,
And could almost be sung as a hymn.

Paul's thoughts on the people of Crete
Expressed openly was indiscrete;
To label them "Lazy"
And "Vicious" was crazy
But it sorted the "weeds" from the "wheat".

Philemon

Philemon, a great friend of St Paul
Had a difficult task to resolve
It concerned young Onesimus
For in quite a mess he was
With no easy way out at all.

Onesimus* was owned as a slave
By Philemon, but freedom he craved,
So away he had run
And was useless (Paul's pun)
To return to Philemon was brave.

*Onesimus, greek = Useful, but as a run-away
slave Onesimus was useless)

But Paul sent him back home to Philemon
With a letter explaining what he'd done
And a vow to repay
Any price he might say
Was the cost of procuring his freedom.

Epistles not written by St Paul

The letter addressed to the Hebrews
Gave much cause for the raising of eyebrows,
The apostle, St Paul
Didn't write it at all,
For it's mystic, symbolic, and highbrow.

St Luke, the beloved physician
Was placed in an awkward position,
For his great buddy Paul
Wasn't healthy at all
And had a recurrent condition.

St Paul asked the Lord, "Would he please
Cure him now of his nasty disease?"
But the Lord said, "My grace
Will suffice in its place,
And will keep you in prayer on your knees."

The letters of James and of John
Teach that faith without love is not on,
While the letters of Peter
Speak of love even sweeter
That was killed without semblance of wrong.

A strange little letter is Jude's
It tells of some spiritual feuds,
And a marked predilection
For God's benediction
Is how the epistle concludes.

The author of "Letters to Hebrews"
Saw quite clearly some things they should see through
For the giants of their faith
Had all run the great race
Resolved that to God they would be true.

The people still known as "The Hebrews"
Got an offer they just could not refuse
Thus The Covenant deed
Through which all may be freed
Was now for Gentiles as well as the Jews.

On the last of his journeys, St. Paul
Told his captors "The boat is too small –
to winter at Crete
Would be wise and discreet
And avoid a bad shipwreck at all".

But the crew and the pilot said "No"
"We can sail round the island in snow
Or whatever the weather
May do, we shall never
Take notice of him," don't you know.

Soon the sea became rougher and rougher
The going got tougher and tougher
But St. Paul reassured them
"No need to take laudanum
Trust in God – he'll see you don't suffer."

The squall became a great storm
The sailors looked scared and forlorn
But Paul, after prayer
Directed them where
The ship could be beached before dawn.

They found that they'd landed in Malta
Paul spoke to them all without falter
Then out from the fire
Came a snake – things looked dire
The snake clung to Paul's wrist, like a halter.

In the end all was well, and St.Paul
Gave thanks to the Lord God of all
Then he swiftly retorted
That God won't be thwarted
By this sort of irritant hassle

The Apocalypse

Whilst on hols in the island of Patmos,
St John had a strange vision that was
Quite a sensation –
A real revelation –
Enough to knock John over backwards.

St John, writes in his revelation
That refiners fire was a solution
"You're not young, you're not old
You're not hot, you're not cold
You're just lukewarm, at risk of pollution".

A message for each of the churches
Gave stability instead of lurches
And a new health and healing
Already fore-seeing
The day when we walk without crutches.

The vision was apocalyptic,
The meaning was really quite cryptic,
It was highly symbolic,
And caused mental colic
If expounded in terms analytic.

So it all ends the way it began,
But instead of a mighty great "Bang",
John tells of a city
Prepared, pure, and pretty,
As a bride all adorned for the Lamb.

And the Lamb takes His place on the throne
And with mortals then God makes His home
Now is Alpha Omega,
And all heaven is eager
To welcome the Lord, and say "Come!"

Post Script

There once was a word from the Lord
That in Limerick format was stored;
Whilst it made easy reading,
The profound deeper meaning
Was by God himself whispered, or roared.

There once was a curate from Clymping,
And Yapton-with-Ford, who'd an inkling
That he could do far worse
Than use Limerick verse
To set all the church people thinking.

A man who read all the four gospels
Saw his faith was all wrapped up in mothballs
And where faith has no works
There's a danger that lurks
In that falling from grace is no soft fall.

So read on then, and see if you find
God's great secret is merely confined
To concise little stories:
Or perhaps rather more is
Just one tale that makes you opine.

The Bible presented in "Limerick"
May well make you laugh – or may make you sick
But God's word's not for joking
The Lord's body was broken:
He died for us all – that's no trick.

A sort of index

…which will tell you where in the Bible is the bit that you want to read…

The Old Testament

The Limerick Bible

Mount Sinai – the giving of the Law (Exodus 20) relating the Law to the Covenant

Mount Sinai, ten commandments, and a golden calf
Exodus 18 – 20 (and 32)
Laws – concerning property, privilege
Food, (clean and unclean)
Ceremonial, associated with the altar; matters of Public Health
Laws in respect of other people
Justice, Mercy, and love

	Exodus
	Leviticus
	Numbers
	Deuteronomy

The Tabernacle, The Ark of the Covenant
A nation of moaners and grumblers
The Law
The rebellion of Korah   Numbers 16
ordination of priests, their duties
Balaam, the donkey, the angel   Numbers 22
and the oracle   Numbers 22ff

The song of Moses,   Deuteronomy 32
The death of Moses   Deuteronomy 34

The promised land – its conquest and occupation by the children of Israel
The Judges
Jael and the tent peg   Judges 4,5

The Prophets	Isaiah
	Jeremiah
+Lamentations	
	Ezekiel
	Daniel
	(Includes some apocalyptic)
The Minor Prophets	Hosea – the unfaithful wife
	Joel – the Day of the Lord
	Amos – the shepherd
	Obadiah – God the judge
	Jonah – the big fish & the gourd
	Micah – God on trial
	Nahum – mayhem at Ninevah
	Habakkuk – the mournful prophet
	Zephaniah – The Royal Prince
	Haggai – the short prophet
	Zechariah – prophet and priest
	Malachi – the last of the OT prophets

The New Testament

Taking an over-view of the Gospel	Matthew
	Mark
	Luke
	John

The Birth of Jesus	Matthew 1,2;
	Luke 1,2
The Music of the Gospel	Luke
The Arrival of the Wise Men	Matthew 2
Jesus, aged 12 goes to the Temple	Luke 2
The Ministry of John the Baptist	Matthew 3,14
	Mark 6
	Luke 3
	John 1
The Baptism of Jesus	Matthew 3
	Mark 1
	Luke 3
	John 1
The Temptation of Jesus	Matthew 3
	Mark 1
	Luke 4
	John 1
The Commencement of Jesus' Early Ministry	Matthew 8
	Mark 1
	Luke 5
	John 2
Jesus Teaches with Authority The Kingdom of Heaven	Matthew 8,9,12
	Mark 6
	Luke 4
	John 5

Changing Fishermen into Fishers of Men
The Twelve are Chosen .... Matthew 10

Mark 3

Luke 10

John 1

The Miracles of Jesus
Water into Wine .... John 2

Peter's Mother-in-Law .... Mark 1
Healing and Forgiveness of Sins .... Mark 2
The Adventure of Bartimaeus .... Mark 10
Healing on the Sabbath .... Mark 3
The Blind See, The Deaf Hear .... Matthew 11
The Lame Walk .... Mark 8
Sick for 38 years .... John 5

Gentiles were Healed too .... Mark 7
Ten Lepers Meet Jesus .... Luke 17
Dead People come Back to Life .... Luke 7
Lazarus .... John 11
The World's Biggest Picnic .... Matthew 14
Jesus Walks on Water .... Matthew 14
One to One with Jesus
Zacchaeus .... Luke 19
The Rich Young Man .... Luke 18
The Woman at the Well .... John 4
Nicodemus by Night .... John 3
Supper with Simon .... Matthew 26

Mark 14

The Limerick Bible

Jesus – The Greatest Story-Teller of All Time
The Stories of the Kingdom of Heaven

The Builders	Matthew 7
The Sower	Matthew 13
	Luke 8
	Mark 4
The Treasure Seekers	Matthew 13
The Good Samaritan	Luke 10
The Lost Sheep	Luke 15
The Lost Coin	Luke 15
The Prodigal (Lost) Son(s)	Luke 15
The Unforgiving Servant	Luke 18
Two Men in the Temple	Luke 18
The Talents	Matthew 18
	Luke 24
Rich Man, Poor Man	Matthew
The Wedding Clothes for the	Mark 21,22
Wedding Breakfast	Luke 14
Yeast	Matthew 13
Wheat and Weeds	Matthew 13
Goats and Sheep	Matthew 13
	Mark 4
Wicked Tenants	Matthew 21
	Mark 12
The Sayings of Jesus	
To Render to Ceasar…or not	Luke 20
The Beatitudes	Matthew 5
	Luke 6
The 'I AM's'	John 4,6,10,11,14,15

166

The Limerick Bible